In My Next Life I'll Get It Right

By

Rosemary

MILD

Magic Island Literary Works • Honolulu, Hawaii • 2021

Covers and interior book design by Larry Mild.
Front Cover Caricature of Rosemary by Seaquist Zipp.

Some of the essays in this collection appeared in the following:
"My Best Move": *Chess Life*, Dec. 2014. Reprinted with permission of
      US Chess.
"In the Drip, Not Grip, of a Dilemma": *Not Everyone's Cup of Tea*, 2013.
"My Blogging, Tweeting Birds": *Truth Quest,* 2014; Petaluma
      (California) Readers Theatre, Sept. 16 & 17, 2011.
"My Black Hat": *Generations*, 2010.
"How I Jeopardized My Sanity": *Scribble*, 2010; *Slow Trains*, Winter
      2008.
"Character Floss": *Washington Post*, Dec. 7, 2009.
"Tulips on Trial": *New Lines from the Old Line State*, 2008.
"*Mea* Kelpie": *Pen in Hand,* Maryland Writers' Association, 2004.
"A Free T-Shirt Has Its Price": *The Publick Enterprise*, July 1997.
"Why the (Former) Redskins Are Always Winners—No Matter What":
      Washington Woman, Oct./Nov. 1995.
Eleven lines in *Roughing It* by Mark Twain, 1872, p. 326. Edition by
      Gibbs Smith, publisher, Layton, Utah, 2017.
Eye of Horus, p. 135; frame, p. 209: Licensed by GoGraph.

Library of Congress Cataloging-in-Publication Data
Mild, Rosemary P.
In My Next Life I'll Get It Right
Mild, Rosemary P.

ISBN 978-0-9905472-8-0
First Edition 2021

10 9 8 7 6 5 4 3 2 1

Dedication

For Larry—my loving husband, best friend, partner

For our beloved grandchildren—
Alena, Craig, Ben, Leah, and Emily

For our precious great-grandson—Kai

For our fabulous daughters—
Jackie and Myrna

Acknowledgments

I could fill an entire volume with the names of all the family members, dear friends, and acquaintances who are loyal fans of our books, essays, and short stories. And you, our readers, are all precious to us and give us the ultimate push to continue our writing.

Special thanks and hugs to:

Sisters in Crime/Hawai'i Chapter and Hawai'i Fiction Writers, for their friendship, encouragement, and advice.

Diane Farkas, our close friend, for her outstanding proofreading skills.

Seaquist Zipp, artist of the caricature of me on the front cover (drawn in 1983). At the time, I was managing editor of *Chemical Times & Trends*, official journal of the Chemical Specialties Manufacturers Association. I was attending a CSMA convention in Chicago. The association had hired artist Seaquist Zipp to create caricatures of the attendees. I am deeply grateful for her cleverness, skill, and humor in portraying me.

Disclaimer

In My Next life I'll Get It Right is a work of personal essays. It contains both real and fictional persons. The points of view expressed herein are those of the author and contain no malice toward any person living or dead.

Table of Contents

Books Coauthored by the Milds

The Dan and Rivka Sherman Mysteries
- Death Goes Postal
- Death Takes A Mistress
- Death Steals A Holy Book
- Death Rules The Night

The Paco and Molly Mysteries
- Locks and Cream Cheese
- Hot Grudge Sunday
- Boston Scream Pie

Adventure/Thrillers
- Cry Ohana
- Honolulu Heat

Short Story Collections
- Murder, Fantasy, and Weird Tales
- The Misadventures of Slim O. Wittz
- Copper and Goldie
- Charlie and the Magic Jug

Science Fiction Novella
- Unto the Third Generation

Also by Rosemary
- Miriam's World—and Mine
- Love! Laugh! Panic! Life with My Mother

Also by Larry
- No Place To Be But Here, My Life and Times

Chapter 1
CONFESSION

I was born in the Chinese Year of the Pig. If I had known this when I was still in my mother's womb, I would have postponed my birth. My husband, Larry, tried to console me. "It's the Year of the Boar. That sounds better."

Pig, boar, what's the difference?

For twenty years we spent our winters in Honolulu, Hawaii, as "snowbirds," renting an apartment, In 2013 we bought our own apartment in the same condo and moved here after more than forty years in Severna Park, Maryland.

I was in our condo elevator with two elderly Japanese ladies. One looked at my Year of the Dog T-shirt and asked, "Were you born in the Year of the Dog?"

I made a sour face, wrinkling my nose: "No. the Year of the Pig."

"Oh, no," she said, her eyes widening in disapproval of my unhappy response. "I'm the Year of the Pig, too. It's gooooood, good people."

I laughed. "Oh, well, if it's us, it must be good."

Luckily, I didn't have the power to postpone my birth, because the very next year in the Chinese Zodiak is the Year of the Rat. No thank you.

Besides, I've discovered some famous pigs that put me in good company. Ralph Waldo Emerson, Stephen King, Wolfgang Amadeus Mozart, Maria Callas, Steven Spielberg, Ernest Hemingway, Humphrey Bogart, Hillary Clinton, Glenn Close, the Dalai Lama, Alex Trebek, and Alfred Hitchcock. And let's not forget Marie Antoinette and Henry VIII.

As a Jewish girl born in the Year of the Pig, my final comment is *oynk oynk!*

Chapter 2
HAWAII ADVENTURES

"...In place of the hurry and bustle and noisy confusion of San Francisco...I moved in the midst of a Summer calm as tranquil as dawn in the Garden of Eden....It was tranced luxury to sit in the perfumed air and forget that there was any world but these enchanted islands.

"It was such ecstasy to dream, and dream—till you got a bite. A scorpion bite....Then came an adjournment to the bed-chamber and the pastime of writing up the day's journal with one hand and the destruction of mosquitoes with the other—a whole community of them at a slap....Then sleep peacefully on the floor till morning."

—**Mark Twain,** writing about Hawaii in *Roughing It*

"Donkey" Tales

*Aloha, Folks! I wrote this essay six months before the
coronavirus pandemic turned our lives upside down.*

I love "Donkey." It's my favorite grocery market, but for so much more than groceries. It's my just-about-everything store. "Donkey" is actually Don Quijote, a full city block on Kaheka Street in Honolulu, a few blocks from Ala Moana mall. I'm possessive of *my* Donkey because it's around the corner from our high-rise condo. I gave it my personal nickname long before I learned that Don Quijote is the biggest discount store in Japan and is nicknamed "Donki" there. But why did a Japanese company give it such a Spanish-sounding name? The company website says the stores were named after the hero in Cervantes' novel *Don Quixote*, "bravely and aggressively offering challenges to the conventional retail industry."

In case you're wondering, I don't work for Donkey. I just like the way it provides entertainment as well as groceries. My biggest problem is avoiding the temptation to buy great stuff I don't need! I jauntily pull my black wire cart around the block, collapse it, and stow it under a store cart to tool around. Not just for food. Maybe a large laminated map of Kauai. Or a filmy jacket with a tiger's head on the back. Or used books and DVDs. Whatever it is, I have adventures—many with unintended consequences.

Until summer 2017, a tiny post office branch nestled on the far left wall. But Donkey underwent a major renovation and the convenient little post office that so many of us depended on did not survive. Missing it the most, I'm guessing, are the shoppers who painstakingly filled out customs forms to mail their holiday gifts to family and friends in Asia and elsewhere abroad.

Once I was in line to buy more sheets of Batman stamps; the graphics were so dramatic and macho. The sheets included small circles of the striking Batman silhouette: black wings spread

3

against a yellow sky. That day I said to Esther, the postal lady: "I'm really enjoying these stamps and the little stickers of the Batman silhouette. I put them on the backs of birthday card envelopes."

Esther gave me a funny look. "They're not stickers. They're stamps!"

Oops! I'd already used twelve; six dollars down the toilet.

A produce man was busy at the wall display of fresh vegetables. He was arranging enormous carrots, almost a foot long, in a dramatic wheel formation. I stopped to look. "What a pretty design!" I said. "You're an artist!" He gave me a tremendous smile.

The next week I stood there ready to buy the longest, fattest carrots on the wheel. I tugged at a choice specimen and found myself face to face with another woman—clutching the other end of the same carrot. We both laughed. What were the odds of that? But she tugged harder and won! Silently, I said goodbye to my prize carrot as she dropped it into a bag.

The aloha spirit seems to reign at Donkey. In line to check out, a young woman in the line next to mine said, "Excuse me, but those bagels have mold on them." She pointed to my clear plastic package standing up in the top tray of the cart. Sure enough. I hadn't noticed the greenish-blue fuzzy patch on one whole-wheat bagel. So kind of her to tell me, especially with her wiggly baby dangling his little feet in the top of the cart. I thanked her and handed it to the checkout clerk, who stowed it away.

Amid all the breathtaking sights on Oahu, who would expect tourists to include Donkey? I always take our visiting family or friends there. And it turns out once is never enough. They insist on going back on their last day to get more Kona coffee, chocolate macadamia nuts, aloha shirts, and souvenirs before returning to the Mainland, even if their departure is just a few hours away. Recently, I was standing with my brother and sister-in-law in the center aisle. We were admiring the *pareos*, the popular beach-wrap sarongs in Hawaiian patterns and splashy colors. "Ninety-nine cents!" I chirped. Ann began painstakingly choosing one for each friend back home in Minnesota. Fifteen minutes later, a local island girl came by with her friend. She checked a price tag. "*Pareos*, $14.95," she announced in a loud voice to her friend. The girls sauntered away. Oh, no! I had been looking at the wrong sign. Ninety-nine cents was for the *tatami* mats on the bottom shelf. Ann piled her large stack of *pareos* back on the shelf—too polite to remind me I'd just wasted fifteen minutes of her precious Donkey time.

My checkout clerk's name tag read "Glenda." I couldn't resist saying to her, "There's a famous actress with your name."

She nodded. "Glenda Jackson."

Then I added, "And the good witch in *The Wonderful Wizard of Oz.*"

"No!" she retorted. "That's Glinda!"

"Oh," I said, embarrassed. "You're right." So much for my recollection of the movie—and the book I read at age twelve. All this with a line of shoppers patiently (and undoubtedly annoyed) waiting to check out.

The hot food deli is so popular that you have to take a number. I was there for their succulent barbecued chicken quarters for our supper, as well as two orders to put in the freezer for Larry: pot roast with gravy and corned beef and cabbage. A lean seventy-ish man handed over his number and asked a lady server behind the counter, "How much?" He was pointing to hamburger patties floating in sauce.

"Four dollars each," she said.

"Fo' dollah fo' one? Goodnight Irene!" He walked away.

When she was wrapping up my order, I said, "You people are much better cooks than I am." She laughed and replied, "We love you!"

The holiday checkout line was long. I began chatting with the young local couple behind me. We smiled at each other, knowing we'd be there a while. "My name is Rosemary," I said. "My husband and I write novels and stories." I handed his wife one of our bookmarks. (Nobody escapes our bookmarks.) She cocked her head toward her husband and said to me: "His name is Boz, B-O-Z."

First of all, you have to know this about me. I'm extremely generous with my opinions. I always have one ready whether anybody wants it or not. I turned to the young man. "Do you know that you have something in common with one of the world's greatest writers?" He looked puzzled.

"Charles Dickens," I said. "In the 1800s he published his stories in the newspaper under his pen name, "Sketches by Boz."

The young man grinned. "That's cool!"

As I turned onto Kaheka Street, hauling my wire cart loaded with my groceries, I heard a voice on my right shouting: "'Bye! Call me when you get off the bus." It was an island woman about five feet tall with tousled gray hair and a cavernous smile that revealed a mouth only half-filled with teeth—all crooked. She said to me, as if I were a friend, "That's my granddaughter. We have lunch once a week before she goes back to Waipahu."

"How nice," I said, surprised but flattered that she wanted to tell me. Not quite sure how to respond, I asked, "What grade is your granddaughter in?"

"She's a senior. She's the first of my fifteen grandchildren to graduate."

"Wow!" I replied, actually dumbfounded. Did she mean high school? College? "Does she have any plans?" I asked cautiously.

"Oh, yes," the lady answered, her expression solemn. "She's going to college. She wants to be a nurse."

"That's wonderful," I said. "You did a good job raising her." I had no idea whether she was responsible in any way for raising her granddaughter, but she did not dispute me.

"Thank you," she said. We walked another few feet, then I stopped at the red light to cross Kaheka. "Good luck to you and your granddaughter," I called out.

She gave me another huge semi-toothy smile and waved as she continued on her way.

In the Produce Department I turned the corner from the Bosc pears and accidentally bumped the edge of another cart, being pushed by a smartly dressed *haole* woman.

"My fault," I said.

"No, *my* fault," she responded.

We parted down different aisles.

Later, I pondered our little cart-bumping exchange. I'm an avid fan of Carol Burnett's incorrigible skits, so my thoughts ran to how she and her sister, Vicky, would have played our responses out.

"My fault."

"No, *my* fault."

"My fault."

"No, *my* fault."

The responses are getting testy.

"Come to think of it," says Vicky, "yes, it *was* your fault!"

"Are you crazy?" Carol shouts. "It was *yours!*"
Hair pulling follows.

I'm a fast walker, always rushing here and there—and a few months ago, I plunged straight into a gruesome Donkey misadventure. In the meat aisle, I tossed packages of frozen chicken into the cart, then rushed back to the dairy case because I'd forgotten my one-percent milk. As I set the half-gallon carton down, I stared in dismay. There sat two small packages of *poke*; they had been packed up specially at the meat and seafood counter, perhaps for an elderly shopper. I had taken the wrong cart to the dairy case! That poor customer! What to do? At 4:30 in the afternoon the store was jammed. Panicked, I pushed my way in frustrating slowness back to the chicken counter and found my own cart where I'd left it. I consoled myself. *Maybe the person went back to the meat and seafood counter, hoping to find their missing poke.* But I was about thirty feet away. I would have to make my way past the hot-meals deli counter, crowded with hungry shoppers in line for their suppers.

So I did the next best thing. I shouted. "Is anyone missing their cart? I took the wrong one by mistake." No one claimed it. Total silence. A lady with a lined face and her hair in a severe bun threw me a wry look of fake disapproval. "You'd better leave—now," she warned.

"You're right," I said. "I'll book a flight to the Mainland tonight."

She laughed.

Oy oy. My hijacking the wrong cart was bad. Really bad. Because it wasn't just a lapse of memory and neglecting to pay attention. It now would rise to the top of my list to atone for on *Yom Kippur*, only a few months away.

At home that night, I phoned a friend and ruefully spilled my story. "Time for Larry to put me out to pasture," I said. "But first I want to choose all the pasture amenities."

My truly wise friend chuckled. "Rosemary, you're already there."

Of course I am.

Honolulu Marathon

Just five months after we moved from Severna Park, I had an exciting adventure on Sunday, December 8, 2013, the day of the annual Honolulu Marathon (26.2 miles). Our son-in-law, Tim Spurrier, was in it (he'd done many; that year he was fifty-five and it was to be his last marathon). Our daughter Myrna and Tim spent the night with us because we lived close to the starting point.

I woke up at 4:00 a.m. Larry awoke just long enough to mumble, "You don't have to do this."

"But I want to!" I said.

We left the house at 4:30 a.m. Together the three of us walked to Ala Moana Boulevard, across from Ala Moana beach park, where the marathon was to start. There were 30,000 participants, thousands from all over the world, including Japan, Africa, and Finland. Half an hour later the loudspeaker came on with the opening ceremony: singing of the national anthem; the Hawaii state song in Hawaiian; a prayer in Hawaiian to bless the participants; and a short speech by the mayor of Honolulu wishing them luck and telling them, "Take care of each other."

Still dark out at exactly 5:00 a.m. the starting gun went off, followed by ten minutes of spectacular fireworks. We couldn't even see the elite runners, who were several blocks ahead of where Tim began (in the group who make it in four to five hours).

A few minutes before the starting gun, I had my own moment of glory. Myrna asked me if I had any cough drops. Tim needed one. I produced a Ricola from my purse. My claim to fame participating in the marathon. Naturally, for weeks after, I bragged about it to anyone who would listen.

It was still very dark out, of course. Myrna and I walked a few blocks to Pensacola Street and sat down on a low wall to see the beginning group: the wheelchair contestants. Their wheelchairs had two huge wheels in the back, a long shaft, and one small wheel in front. They were escorted by special cyclists with lights on their foreheads and handlebars to provide protection for them. The strength of the competitors in these wheelchairs, and their speed, was awe-inspiring.

After an hour, when the sun started coming up, Myrna and I walked back to our apartment for breakfast. Later she drove to a mall, parked, and waited for Tim to pass by. She actually found him and walked five miles with him (but not as a contestant), then he ran the rest of the way to the finish line. Each participant wore a number with a chip in it, so I logged onto the event and was able to track Tim's progress at several points, and at the end. He finished in six hours, #10,775. He was a little disappointed, because he's done it many times in four hours, among the first 3,000, but he was still impressive, considering that he now had a health issue—the reminder of a broken hip years ago. Larry and I were proud of him, and I was exhilarated to be part of the adventure.

My Best Move

I just finished a suspense novel called *The Eight* by Katherine Neville—about a priceless but cursed chess set once owned by Charlemagne. Can such a curse migrate and invade the psyche of a player centuries later?

A few years ago, wintering in Honolulu, I got a chance to play chess with our nineteen-year-old grandson Ben. We were at our daughter's house celebrating Chanukah. All twelve of us were groaning from too many latkes, the traditional potato pancakes.

The chessboard was glass with exquisite crystal pieces. I panicked. *How can I do this? What if I drop one and it shatters?*

It was my first chess game in twenty-five years. I concentrated mightily, stayed focused, and after an hour, I had maneuvered a clear advantage. I was primed for my next move....

* * * *

In the early 1960s my ex-husband taught me the game in our New York City walkup with its gray floorboards and the bathtub in the kitchen. I learned the basics, but there my patience played its own end game. He studied famous grand-master strategies, like the Panov-Botvinnik Attack, the Nimzo-Indian Defense, and the Queen's Gambit. I didn't.

Years later, I was newly divorced, raising my small daughter in a desolate Maryland suburb forty miles from Washington, D.C. As a career editor, I joined the National Press Club, assuming it would generate a social life for me. The Club had 4,000 members and a zillion activities, including a chess tournament. *I'll meet people!* How many members entered? Six. Including me.

My first game was against a Norwegian, the Washington correspondent of an Oslo newspaper. His office was in the National Press Building itself, just a few floors below the Club. Our game lasted twenty minutes. I gave myself a litany of excuses for losing. The hour's drive from my job in Baltimore—in the dark through pounding rain. The Club's game room, where men were hunched over tables, puffing away on their cigarettes, while I was trying to focus on the chess board through eye-tearing smoke.

My next opponent was the retired Washington correspondent of Radio Free Europe. In the living room of his upscale townhouse, the mahogany chess table sat on an Oriental rug. He placed a notebook and pen next to the board. "I like to record every move," he said.

We played in total creepy silence for two hours. I'd *never* played a game this long. My brain wanted a vacation. Suddenly, surprising even myself, I took his queen. Now was the moment for me to dig in, strategize, and move in for the kill.

Abruptly, he pushed his chair back from the table. "Time for lunch," he announced. He'd prepared it himself, a rich stew plus slabs of buttered cornbread.

Half an hour later, thoroughly stuffed, my eyelids drooped. I tried to focus as we resumed our game. I had taken his queen. I had the power! By all rights I should have won. But I didn't. Hey! Was that his strategy? If you lose your queen, stop the game and serve a huge, high-carb lunch?

This wasn't the first time I'd defeated myself. Often against my ex-husband I'd fade in the end game. I just don't have the killer instinct.

I had one more opportunity to reverse my kamikaze course in the tournament. My third opponent was Gilbert Grosvenor, retired editor-in-chief of *National Geographic.* At his gracious home in Bethesda, Maryland, we sat down to play. Mrs. Grosvenor brought us tea and a plate of hard Italian cookies—biscotti, meant to be dunked. But I didn't know that. I just gnawed at the edges, filling my mouth with crumbs. I saw a diabolical pattern taking shape. Food. Was this any way to muster the killer instinct?

* * * *

Back to our Chanukah party in Honolulu. I shifted my brain into overdrive and made my next move.

Suddenly, Ben leaped up to his full six-foot height. "Hah-hah!" he shouted. "It's a stalemate! Dad! I got a stalemate against Grandma!"

He did indeed. Instead of pushing him to the wall by making my final move and announcing "Checkmate," I had left his king boxed in with nowhere to go. Of course, that mistake officially created a draw.

The killer instinct continues to elude me. But, *boy*, did I make our grandson happy.

Valentine's Day: Big-Time Stressor

February 14, 2020. I was coming out of my Physical Therapy appointment in an office building on Valentine's Day. Standing at the elevator was a fortyish woman, pleasant-looking, embracing a huge bouquet of pink rosebuds and white baby's breath. Sticking out was a Mylar balloon saying, "Happy Valentine's Day."

"The bouquet is beautiful," I said.

"Thank you," she replied. "This year he remembered."

THIS YEAR HE REMEMBERED. Her sentence thundered in my brain, creating a whole scenario. Last year he must have forgotten and she'd given him hell for it. Or sulked for three days. Or maybe she pulled a Carol Burnett skit.

"What's wrong, hon?" Harvey asks.

"Nothing!" Carol squeaks.

So this year the poor guy decided he'd better make up for it. How much anxiety had it cost him days in advance? Timing it for delivery to her office, where she could proudly evoke the envy of less lucky coworkers.

Which makes me think about Valentine's Day. In reality, for many people it's a huge stressor. Spouses and significant others wrack their brains to remember the date and figure out just the right thing, whether they can afford it or not.

On TV you can't escape the guilt. The marketers are out in full force. Think how many businesses count on our guilt for immense profits. The chocolate industry, the jewelers, the florists.

So what do Larry and I buy each other for Valentine's Day?

Nothing. We just say "I love you"—as we do every day, more than once because it makes us happy. Every day is Valentine's Day for us.

Larry also proposes to me every day.

"Will you marry me?"

"Yes!" I say. After all, it's appropriate. We've only been married thirty-three years.

Smoothies
Pre-COVID Report

Every year we spend 2-½ days (often spring and fall) in a booth at Blaisdell Exhibition Hall to sell our books at the Hawaii Holiday Gift & Craft Fair. Along one wall is a smoothie vendor whom I've been visiting for years, and yet I can't remember his booth's official name.

But he remembers me. I may not have come there for a whole year. Still, as I approach his booth, he always looks up, smiles, and says, "Two strawberry-banana, no whipped cream." Exactly right! What an excellent businessman.

* * * *

Just outside Don Quijote's doors, all along the wall as you approach, there are inviting food vendors. They're all take-out except two, both eat-in, one Hawaiian, the other Korean.

One vendor sells smoothies. A long time ago, I ordered one with tapioca "bubbles." I had no idea what bubbles were. I only discovered them when I was handed my drink: tiny black gelatinous balls lying on the bottom. I chewed on one—tasteless, and left the others in the bottom, happily tossing them out after finishing the drink.

Once recently, just once, I ordered a strawberry smoothie from the same vendor, this time no bubbles. I took a sip and set the cover straight as I pulled my own wire cart loaded with groceries. I walked the block and around the corner to our condo. Wedging the smoothie in a corner at the top of the groceries, I opened my purse to dig out my keys, then went up to the fifteenth floor. As I inserted the key with both hands, opened the door, and stepped inside, I noticed something bad. A pink trail of smoothie had followed me into our front hall. I looked down and for the first time noticed that the plastic cover was cockeyed. I had not secured it tightly enough after taking a sip when I left the booth.

After mopping it up with paper towels, I needed to go back down to the lobby to get our day's mail. In the elevator, to my distress I discovered little pink smoothie puddles on the elevator floor! As it reached the lobby and the doors opened, the full impact of my carelessness hit me. There was a trail of smoothie puddles all across the lobby's freshly waxed floor, from the side door where I had entered to the elevator. "Oh, no," I said aloud, "look what I did!" I was talking to the guard, a lovely young woman named Deanna sitting at her Guard's Desk across the room. She said kindly, "Don't worry, I've already called Maintenance." And there came dear Danny, with a mop and pail, ready to clean up my pink blobs.

This is not good, I decided. *Maybe I should make my own smoothies.* Our daughter Jackie gave me her smoothie machine. I bought a package of frozen strawberries and bananas and added milk. Not sweet enough. At our next book signing at Blaisdell I consulted my smoothie man. "Apple juice," he advised. That tasted better. But next time I shopped, the only frozen fruit available was a berry mix: strawberries, blueberries, raspberries, and blackberries. Larry and I shared the smoothie, but after a few sips, we found ourselves with mouthfuls of seeds. That was a year ago. We haven't used the machine since. I just returned it to Jackie.

Kindness

After dinner with our family at the Old Spaghetti Factory, Larry and I returned home to a disconcerting sight: a fire engine in front of our condo building. Nobody was around to tell us why. We parked in our normal garage stall on the third floor and headed to the elevators that would take us to our apartment on the fifteenth floor. As always, Larry walked heavily on two canes, required after disappointing spinal surgery four years earlier. At the two elevators I pressed the Up button. Nothing happened.

A young woman with her two daughters approached and told us, "The elevators aren't working. Both are out." From what she had learned, power to our building was accidentally cut, possibly by workmen doing a repair in the neighbor-hood. No time had been set for when the elevators would be operating. We were facing twelve flights of steep concrete stairs.

"Hey, Larry," I said, "we could go across the street to the Pagoda Hotel and spend the night."

"No, I'm gonna walk up."

The woman had a slender, gaunt body, dark hair, and keen, intelligent eyes. "I'm Teresa," she said. "We're here from the Philip-pines visiting my sister on the twelfth floor." She faced Larry with a worried look. "I'll be happy to help you up the stairs."

"No thanks," he said, "I can manage."

Teresa told us her daughters were nine and fourteen. They said goodbye and quickly mounted the stairs. Larry and I began slowly, steadily trudging up. He had cleverly named his canes "Cane" and "Able" and now held them both in his left hand so he could hold onto the banister with his right. Halfway up, he sat down on a step to rest and catch his breath. Suddenly, Teresa and her girls came trotting back down to us. She handed each of us a water bottle! They followed us slowly up the stairs, but did not depart on the twelfth floor. Teresa insisted on accompanying us all the way to our apartment to be sure Larry got safely inside.

We invited them in and gave them two of our books plus bookmarks: our Hawaii suspense novel *Cry Ohana*—the hero is a fourteen-year-old boy; and our mystery *Locks and Cream Cheese,* because it has a clever nine-year-old girl. Nice coincidence. We inscribed them to Teresa and the girls, Sofia and Josephine. Teresa was thrilled.

So were we, touched by her kindness. And what a role model for her daughters.

The Disappearing Paper

We're long-time subscribers to the *Honolulu Star-Advertiser*, and one of my great pleasures is opening our front door every morning at 7:00 a.m. to pick up our paper and set it on the table for my breakfast reading. Larry doesn't have to share it. He reads his *Washington Post* on his iPad at the kitchen table.

It's extremely rare for me to discover an empty space where the paper should be; delivery is usually around 4:30 a.m. A few times when our door was missed I always chalked it up to the delivery person absent-mindedly missing us. I'd call the automated *Star-Advertiser* hot line and request a re-delivery. It would always come shortly.

But something weird began to happen. The paper was missing more frequently. Our friends directly across the hall also subscribed and I always found theirs right in place. But not ours. A shiver shot through me. Is somebody who lives on our floor stealing our paper? A couple of doors down the hall from us people came and went, and I wondered....

A *Star-Advertiser* customer service person sounded puzzled when I called to complain, but she never questioned me.

Then one day when the paper didn't appear, our friend across the hall was on his way out.

"Did you get your paper this morning?" I asked.

"Sure," he said.

"We didn't get ours," I said.

He hesitated a moment, frowned, and added, "When I picked up ours at 6:30 I saw yours was there, too. Somebody must've taken it."

Yes. Somebody on our floor was filching my newspaper! What to do? I could think of only one solution: beat whoever it was to it. My anxiety-ridden brain stepped in, cooperating, waking me up automatically around 5:30 every morning. I would stumble out of bed in my thigh-length nightshirt, open our heavy steel apartment door, and find our newspaper Right Where It Should Be. I'd pick it up and lay it on the kitchen table. This went on for two months. It wasn't an optimal solution. I felt like I was being kept hostage to the filcher because I couldn't always go back to sleep until our alarm rang. Sometimes I'd just lie in bed cuddling up with my pillow, but my head whirling with unwelcome thoughts, my heart doing a dance of relief, but wishing my body would leave me alone and let me sleep!

One afternoon I opened our door to go downstairs for the mail, and I saw a muscular young man emerge from a nearby apartment across the hall. He was pulling two large suitcases to the elevator. My thought was: *Going on vacation or moving out? Seems like a lot of luggage for a vacation.* I did not take the same elevator. The next morning, to test matters out, I waited until 6:00 a.m., then 6:30, and then 7:00, when my alarm rang. I opened the front door. My paper awaited me!

A few days later, a group of four roommates moved into that apartment. I have never had a problem since.

One morning I happened to meet our across-the-hall friend as I was headed out. I told him my observation of the neighbor with the luggage. "My paper seems to be safe now."

"Yes," he nodded. "I'm aware of that."

I had told my sad story to our Site Manager, a smart, sympathetic man, and I reported what appeared to be a happy ending.

"Great!" he said. "I'll call the *Star-Advertiser* and let them know so they don't blame it on their delivery man."

'Thank you," I said. "That's a wonderful idea."

Ladies' Rooms

We were having dinner at the Outrigger Reef Waikiki Beach Resort. Inside a ladies room stall, I pulled the sterilized toilet seat cover out of the dispenser and tried to arrange it on the seat. I can never do those things right. Do I break it apart and fit it on or just leave it in a circle? No matter what I do, it always sinks into the toilet bowl before I've even had a chance to sit down. This one didn't. Instead it chose to fall on the floor and float into the stall next to mine. *Oh dear*, I thought, *this is embarrassing. And I'm littering, too!* But then a hand in the next stall reached down and picked it up. I could hear it being crunched into a ball to throw away.

"Thank you!" I said.

"You're welcome!" she replied. And we both broke into a hearty chuckle.

We didn't get to meet face to face over the sinks. Nevertheless…sisterhood.

Often my trips to ladies' rooms collide with my hopeless sense of direction. It's really bad—especially in a restaurant like Buca di Beppo in Honolulu, with its twists and turns to its various dining areas. If I go to the ladies' room I need a GPS to get back to our table. Servers rushing from the kitchen carrying dinners see me walking around in a daze and kindly stop to direct me.

A Driving Disaster

February 17, 2005. I had attended my Jazzercise class downtown at Royal Elementary School, and I was driving home in the dark at 7:00 p.m. My endorphins had kicked in. I was "wired" in the best sense from my workout, and now from the exhilaration of listening to Hayden's *Water Music* on Hawaii Public Radio.

Driving down Ward Avenue the light was green, and I was ready to turn left. I heard a deep male voice from another car yell to me: "Hey!" I paid no attention. The light turned yellow. I kept turning left.

As I turned, I discovered to my horror that I had turned left onto Beretania Street, a five-lane, one-way road—*and I was going the wrong way!* Going the wrong way on one of the most heavily traveled roads in congested Honolulu.

How to extricate myself from this nightmare? I immediately moved to the far right lane. The car coming toward me slowed to a stop and the cars in the next three lanes also stopped to allow me to do a fast U-turn, which I did. I felt sick.

Suddenly a police car with blue lights flashing was following me. Of course. I pulled into the far left lane near the State Library, stopped, and rolled down my window. I unzipped the wallet pocket of my purse, ready to take out my driver's license.

The police officer approached. "Hi," he said.

"Hi, officer. You saw me."

"Yes. Are you from here?"

"No, but we're snowbirds, here for the winter. This is a rental car. I lost my bearings. I was coming home from Jazzercise and got distracted. I should have turned left on Kinau. Some very nice drivers stopped for me to turn around."

He nodded. "You missed your turn."

He had his ticket pad in his hand and opened it.

"Officer, I'm terribly sorry. It shouldn't have happened. I know better." I was totally prepared to accept a ticket.

He closed his ticket pad. "Just be careful from now on."

I thanked him. I drove slowly down Beretania, turned left on Punchbowl Street, and left again at King, managing to get home without another crisis.

The impact of what I had done swept over me and I felt like crying. I trembled. God had been watching over me and saved me from a horrible accident, not only to myself, but from having a head-on collision and killing other people.

What happened was, unfortunately, rather typical of me. I got so wrapped up in the beautiful classical music that I literally went on automatic pilot. My thoughts drifted and I did not pay attention to what I was doing. God gave me a break—He delivered me from a disaster that would have affected every driver around me and their loved ones.

It was a wake-up call.

How I Jeopardized My Sanity

Jeopardy! **is my favorite TV show. I wrote this essay in 2008, and it was published in** *Scribble* **and online in** *Slow Trains*. **I include it here in affectionate memory of Alex Trebek, who died at age eighty on November 8, 2020. He was a brilliant and engaging host who established a warmth toward and personal interest in every contestant.**

The Hilton Hawaiian Village, a sumptuous resort in the heart of Waikiki, used to be my favorite haunt. It always beckoned like a Siren in *The Odyssey*, with its beachside music, luscious restaurants, exotic wildlife, and Friday night fireworks. But now, every time I set a sandal on its turf, I suffer pangs of regret.

It's the Internet's fault. The Internet makes everything too easy. *Click, click* and *voila!* You've committed yourself to some reckless venture—like signing yourself up to be a contestant on *Jeopardy!* An announcement during the show had said the team was coming to Honolulu for three days of testing at the Hilton Hawaiian Village. Larry and I were "snowbirds" in 2006, wintering in Honolulu, so how could I not leap at this chance to join the brainy wannabes?

Today you can take the test online. Not so in 2006. I would have to bodily appear. I sat at my computer, *Click, click*, and recklessly applied. The very next day I received a response. "Congratulations! You have been selected for an appointment." *Oh my God, what have I done?*

Jeopardy! is the second longest-running game show on television (after *Wheel of Fortune*), and the format is unique, the reverse of the usual quiz show. A player selects a category and dollar value from the list offered. Host Alex Trebek presents contestants with a clue in the form of an answer. The contestant must respond in the form of a question, preceded by "What is..." or "Who is..." or "Where is..."

I'm addicted to *Jeopardy!* Larry and I record it and watch

it every night before going to bed. But I used to be a whole lot quicker in our living room than I am now. I'm convinced that the most successful contestants possess four qualities: photographic memories; a life-long happy obsession with accumulating knowledge; nerves of titanium; and lightning reflexes—not only mental, but physical, meaning a masterful thumb on the response button. My DNA does not include any of these skills.

I accepted the email invitation, noting that we were going back to our home in Severna Park, Maryland, on April 1. *Good*, I thought, *our departure schedule will kill the appointment and I can relax.* But no. The very next day, I got my marching orders. Be at the Hilton Hawaiian Village on February 21, 2006, at 11:30 a.m. The test would consist of fifty questions. I was to come dressed in what I'd wear if I were chosen as a contestant. But the invitation warned: "Even if you pass the test, we cannot guarantee that you will be invited to do the show."

That night I woke up at 2:00 a.m. and couldn't go back to sleep. I realized I had only one month to LEARN EVERYTHING. In the morning, I called Barnes & Noble to get a book, any book, dealing with past *Jeopardy!* shows. They didn't have one. A teacher friend told me to buy a trivia book. I literally ran to the mall, four blocks away, and came home with a *2006 Time Almanac*.

Next, back to the evil Internet that got me into this in the first place. I logged onto links of former *Jeopardy!* champions. The crosscurrents of advice were akin to entering the Bermuda Triangle. I found three pages of instructions on how to handle the response button. "You must wait until Alex has finished giving the answer or you get locked out for a few seconds. Activating the button requires pressure. Rest your hand holding the button device on the podium to steady it. Or you can hold it in your hand." I learned of a three-day champion who practiced at home using a toilet paper spring roller.

Another champion offered a sample test, which "should take ten minutes." I was in such a hurry to take it that I forgot to write down numbers one through fifty in advance. So I wasted time, fretted about it, and got only twenty-six right. The minimum is thirty-five, or 70 percent.

As Larry and I splashed around our apartment pool, he offered to drill me on the U.S. capitals. *A no brainer*, I thought. But I sucked in a mouthful of chlorinated water as I discovered I only knew about half. Topeka, Kansas? Lansing, Michigan? Helena, Montana? Pierre, South Dakota? Salem, Oregon? I was smarter in eighth grade.

The almanac became an extension of my body. I even took it into the bathroom, one of my favorite reading places, and set it on the Formica counter. (Sorry, Wilkie Collins, your *Woman in White* will have to wait a month.) In bed that night, I propped the almanac on my belly, preparing for my first real cram session. It was 11 o'clock. Larry laughed. "Think you'll be finished by morning?" He dropped off to sleep. I didn't. After memorizing the first twelve U.S. presidents in order, I turned off my light. So much for cramming.

I woke up at 6:00 a.m. in a panic. Was it Tyler-Polk-Taylor or Taylor-Polk-Tyler? A peek at the almanac: right the first time. Sunday breakfast had always meant a leisurely hour with two newspapers. But not now. I found a story about the world's most horrendous dictators. "Better memorize those," Larry said. Of the twenty pictured, I only knew three. Instead of my honey-wheat bagel, I digested women heads of state: Ellen Johnson Sirleaf, Liberia; Michelle Bachelet, Chile. Opening the almanac, I spilled guava jelly on the chemical elements.

In the following weeks, I studied Verdi operas, Super Bowl winners, Irish authors, mixed drinks, and the tallest peak in the Andes: Aconcuaga in Argentina. I started memorizing country capitals. Angola: Luanda. Azerbaijan: Baku. Democratic Republic of the Congo: Kinshasa. Republic of Congo: Brazzaville. Djibouti: Djibouti.

The day before my appointment I made an ominous discovery. The ocean of facts I absorbed a month ago—the facts that surged into my head like the waves on Sunset Beach—had now receded to some distant swell where the sea turtles live.

Yikes! What to wear? I always critique the women contestants' clothes. I note what colors work well, what styles, what makes a woman look anorexic or chubby or drab or gorgeous. I set the parameters. Nothing ruffled, too frou-frou. No flashy jewelry, too distracting. Another jaunt to the mall. I bought an aqua jacket, black pants, and plain camisole— one of that year's "with-it" ensembles. Plus arty silver earrings to look younger. I hadn't seen a contestant who looked my age since *Jeopardy!* abandoned the senior tournaments—perhaps because they couldn't find enough seniors who remembered things. That night I ruefully realized my three-hour shopping excursion was wasteful. I should have been studying!

"J" Day. February 21, 11:00 a.m., At the Hilton Hawaiian Village I rolled into the parking garage and started walking. I had no idea where to go in this opulent complex set on twenty-two acres. So I whispered the magic word to the bell captain. "*Jeopardy!*" He smiled sympathetically and directed me to the Tropics Showroom. This was the third and last day of testing in Honolulu (about fifty of us each day). In the anteroom, a few test takers stood about, shifting from foot to foot. There were no chairs, no receptionist to take our names, no Security to frisk us. A sign said, "The doors will open at 11:30, not a minute before."

I left the room, strolled past a swimming pool filled with sunburning tourists, and visited the jungle garden. The flamingoes ignored me; they were too busy balancing on one leg. They looked so improbable, so pristine. Pristine? *Now I've done it.* I forgot to put on deodorant after my shower. It was 11:15, too late to find a sundries shop. *I'll be disqualified!* I visualized a sumo-size guard blocking the testing room doorway, growling at me: "Sorry. The correct response is "What is Lady Speed Stick?""

I returned to the Tropics anteroom at 11:22, perspiration beading up in my misbehaving armpits. No one socialized; everyone looked agitated. Some of the men stood about in their dignified suits and ties; others slouched in jeans or cargo pants and

T-shirts. I compared the women's outfits to mine. A young woman in a sleeveless blouse had flamboyant tattoos covering every inch of her arms. *If she makes it onto the show, will they require her to wear long sleeves?* I'd never seen a tattooed contestant. An Asian woman carrying a briefcase was wearing an aqua jacket, the same color as mine. She nodded, but didn't invite conversation, and that was fine with me. *Concentrate*, I reminded myself. *Focus*. My psychoanalyst father once told me, "You woolgather, you daydream." I know, but I've never figured out how to stop.

At precisely 11:30, fifty-five of us were ushered in; we merely had to show our invitation at the door. There were no tables, no lecture-hall chairs with pop-up writing surfaces. Just small velvet chairs squeezed together, as if we were attending a Revive-Your-Marriage retreat. On each seat there was a test paper with cardboard backing. The man in front of me had a large head and even bigger hair. I couldn't see the screen well. The screen was the old-fashioned, home-movie type.

A young man "coach," for lack of a better word, greeted us in an upbeat voice. He asked if anyone had taken the test before. Six hands went up. He ran us through a casual sample show, flashed on the screen with the categories and dollar amounts. We raised our hands to answer. We were instructed *not* to write down "What is?" Just our responses.

Finally, the test. No categories to select, no dollar amounts. Just random answers in miscellaneous categories, called out to us orally, with about eight seconds to write each response. We began. The first answer I should have known, but I didn't. It seemed everyone else did. The second and fourth I did know. The third and fifth, I've known for years, but my brain blocked! *Traitor! Rat!* I scribbled a note next to each blank, a reminder so I could come back to it. By number forty, I was losing my concentration. I wrote only half the response to the last clue.

"That's it, friends, time's up! Pass your papers in." I took the ones handed me from my left and passed them to the woman on my right. And now I remembered the questions to numbers three and five. I wanted to fill them in, but I didn't, fearing the coach would see me and think I was copying another person's paper.

"The tests will be graded in twenty minutes," he told us. "But while you're waiting, we have a surprise for you. Alex Trebek!" Alex strode to the front of the room wearing an orange aloha shirt and slacks. Relaxed and charming, sincere and unaffected. One man raised his hand and asked, "Why did you shave off your mustache?" Alex looked at him in mock surprise and said, "*You* don't have a mustache." Everyone laughed. He talked about the test. "Don't be discouraged if you don't pass. Some contestants took the test six and seven times before passing." Good grief! The test cannot be taken more than once a year. Those applicants kept trying for six or seven years?

At last, the verdict. Alex was handed a small sheaf of test papers. He studied them and announced the names of those who passed. Six men and two women (about the same number and ratio of men to women as on the two previous days). In the next hour, the lucky eight would go through a mock show and short interview. Alex said, "If you don't exhibit personality in the interview, you won't be invited on the show. And if you're not called within one year, you won't get called at all."

About 25,000 hopefuls audition each year. Only 400 make it onto the show.

The coach told the rest of us "Goodbye and good luck" and then warned: "Everything we said here stays in this room." I assumed he meant everything significant that wasn't already on the show's website.

I slunk back into our apartment, took off my trendy jacket, and confessed to Larry: "I failed the test." I ached to reveal all the answers and questions. "But we're not allowed."

Eager to help, Larry asked, "Did you sign anything?"
"No."
"Then you're not liable. You can say whatever you want."

I gasped. "No, I can't!" I visualized Alex Trebek finding out that I had blabbed, and gruesome images flooded my brain. He'd roar: "Get that woman's name and address, her fingerprints, her voice print, her DNA. Tell her never to darken the *Jeopardy!* testing doors again. And one more thing. Get her pen back."

That nightmarish thought did it. My lips were eternally zipped. Because that was my one tangible reward: the ballpoint pen given to each of us to take the test. It's royal blue and silver, with JEOPARDY! emblazoned in red block letters. And I am never giving it up.

Give Us This Day Our Daily Bride

Oh, the bliss of pre-COVID-19 life. Here I report on one joyous month in 2007.

Tokyo has its Meiji Shrine, with its stately Shinto wedding processions. The Mormon Temple in Salt Lake City holds as many as forty weddings a day. But we in Honolulu have Magic Island. There's truly something magical about it, especially for brides. And for those of us who discover them.

Larry and I took our heart-healthy walks there several times a week. It didn't take long for us to notice white limousines, with brides and grooms spilling out and heading to every scenic spot on Magic Island. On eight consecutive walks, from January 24th to February 21st, we saw thirteen brides and grooms, always accompanied by a photographer. And perhaps another person, maybe the bride's mother. Most often, they had come solely for picture-taking. Occasionally, for an actual ceremony. Once we saw eight brides in one afternoon!

Magic Island, my favorite locale in all of Hawaii, is a small peninsula extending from the parking lot to the ocean at Ala Moana beach park. Under umbrella-shaped monkeypod trees, locals gather, especially on weekends, for celebrations or maybe just feasting and *talking story*. Aromas of barbecue and teriyaki sauce tease our nostrils. The day after Christmas, the training wheel brigade emerges as toddlers test their new tricycles. Oceanside, on any given day, we might see a hulking container ship; high school paddlers racing their outriggers; a fisherman packing three squirming octopi into his bucket; Diamond Head, jade green after days of downpours. What could be a more perfect setting for wedding pictures?

During one particular afternoon in 2007, a barefoot couple stood on the beach at the water's edge. The groom rolled up his fine gray trousers. The bride hoisted her wedding gown up and bunched it around her waist; it looked like a white organdy inner tube. Holding hands, they waded into the ocean.

Another young couple frolicked in full wedding regalia; the groom galloped along the beach, carrying his bride piggyback.

A bride and groom joyously lay flat on their bellies in the sand—she in her flowing gown, he in his white suit. The photographer also lay on his belly taking their pictures.

Another bride and groom stood on the skinny promontory facing Diamond Head. Suddenly, he scooped her up in his arms. No, he did not toss her into the surging waves.

On one afternoon near dusk, winds were gusting at forty miles an hour. Charcoal-gray clouds blanketed the sky. Never mind. Near the lagoon wedding preparations were under way. Three bridal couples, three photographers. Party helpers bustled about arranging folding chairs and tiki torches decorated with white bows. Preparing for a sunset ceremony—except there was no sun. A small table set with a white cloth held six champagne glasses and a vase of orchids. We hoped they would get to complete the ceremony before the rains. As we walked past, a sharp gust blew the glasses and vase onto the grass.

"If only I had my camera," I told Larry. From that day on, I carried it attached to my belt. This was ten years before I graduated to an iPhone. It was a modest digital Canon PowerShot A400, with a small zoom. I took my pictures from a discreet distance, not wanting to invade the couples' privacy. But, hey, did they have any expectation of privacy? Not on your life, I assured myself. Not at the most popular beach park on all of Oahu. One night I Googled "Magic Island" and discovered whole businesses dedicated to wedding photography. Now it all made sense.

* * * *

Sadly, COVID-19 is destroying all the fun—and the wedding photography business. One company reported last June that they had sixty-eight cancellations in the month of May alone!

When the COVID finally ends, will all the postponed weddings be re-scheduled? Will there be a great surge of photography appointments re-booked? I can see it now. Hundreds of limos lined up in the re-opened parking lot. Brides and grooms eagerly emerging, thundering onto Magic Island like wolf packs, all vying for the most scenic spots. Hordes of wedding couples pushing each other out of their way. The brides in their white satin pumps hobbling to the sea wall, surging forward in such mobs that they will topple off the wall, still clutching their bouquets, and fall onto the lava boulders below. Then be carried out to sea by the receding waves—and rescued by lifeguards in tuxedos. Will there be brides and grooms parasailing in their wedding garb? Will there be paddleboard weddings with the officiator and guests each on their own paddleboard? Will a tugboat chug by, towing a wedding party on a barge as salty vows are said?

We fervently hope that day will come soon. And when it does, Larry and I will be there to witness the wedding revival.

Pearl Harbor and Punchbowl

In November, 2007, while visiting friends in Annapolis, we chatted about our snowbird adventures in Honolulu. The wife, whom I'll call "Susan," told us a startling story. Her father was a Navy commander on a cruiser docked in Pearl Harbor—on December 7, 1941, the Sunday morning of the Japanese invasion. His ship was bombed. None of the crew survived.

Susan said, "I never knew my father. I was in my mother's womb at the time." She couldn't continue. Through tears, she finally said, "I've never been to Hawaii. Isn't there a military cemetery in Honolulu? Do you think you'd find his name someplace there?"

"Very likely," Larry said. The two of us jumped at the idea of pursuing the research, doing something special for her.

The National Memorial Cemetery of the Pacific is known locally as "Punchbowl." Its bowl-shaped crater lies in the middle of an extinct volcano on 116.5 acres. This military cemetery is located high up, overlooking Oahu on Puowaina Drive, which means "Consecrated Hill" or "Hill of Sacrifice." More than 40,000 graves are arranged in concentric circles. Punchbowl was established to honor the efforts of American Armed Forces in the Pacific during World War II and the Korean War, then expanded to include the Vietnam War. At the very top of the staircase, a statue of Lady Columbia gazes down on the walls of names, representing the grieving mothers who lost their children during times of war.

On December 11, 2007, taking both our cameras, we drove up to Punchbowl to locate Susan's father's name. We stopped at the small building where there were two locator machines (to find a particular grave). There were also handouts, including a diagram of the layout of the graves and the Courts—the fifteen-foot walls —arranged like ten small courtyards. Etched in the walls are the alphabetized names of over 28,000 soldiers, sailors, and Marines who didn't survive.

After searching a few minutes without success, a man in a hard hat working on a ladder climbed down and offered to help us. He was a Vietnam veteran, Hawaiian, and his name was Gordon Ka'aiakamanu. He told us his name meant "birdfeeder." He led us to the proper Court on the other side of the long, wide staircase, and there we found the name of Susan's father. We choked up; it suddenly felt very personal to us. His name was quite high on the wall. We took pictures, but we also had planned to do a rubbing for her. We brought tracing paper and purple and blue crayons. But Gordon told us there was a much better way. He called the office. Within minutes, a staff member drove up with a soft pencil and huge piece of paper just for this purpose, with sticky-back on the left and right sides so it would stay against the wall during the rubbing. Then Gordon moved his ladder and climbed up to do the rubbing for us. He did a great job, even though the wind was blowing and Larry had to stand on tiptoe to hold one corner down. Then I climbed up and tried to do my own rubbing with our blue crayon. Lousy idea. Wrong medium. The result was clumsy and not aesthetic.

We thanked Gordon profusely and he agreed to pose for a picture with me. Fortunately, we always keep a supply of our books in the car. We presented him with autographed copies of my memoir *Miriam's Gift: A Mother's Blessings—Then and Now* and our second Paco and Molly mystery, *Hot Grudge Sunday.*

Finally, behind the statue of Lady Columbia we explored the towering semi-circular wall, maybe a hundred feet long, that tells the story of all our wars in the Pacific—in marble and mosaic. Text, illustrations, maps. An amazing presentation.

We sent Susan a mailing tube containing the rubbing and a priority package containing a CD that Larry made of our photos and a letter describing our deeply emotional experience.

Delivering Meals on Wheels
Thanksgiving Day in Honolulu

In 2008, for the first time, I joined our daughter Jackie and granddaughter Leah to deliver Meals on Wheels. Leah drove Jackie's Dodge Durango SUV. The two of them (and Alena before she went off to college) did this every year, and often on Christmas Day, too.

We took the freeway and exited at School Street. In the Lanikila School neighborhood, women and girls held up signs directing us to the Meals on Wheels pickup location. Jackie, already a signed-up volunteer, was handed a pink card with her assigned names and addresses. At the pickup area, several men loaded boxes and bags into the Durango way-back (as Jackie calls her trunk).

Each recipient was to get a partitioned container of turkey with gravy, green beans, and mashed potatoes; a dinner roll; a slice of pumpkin pie; and a bottle of water. Plus something new that year: a bag containing sundries such as a roll of toilet paper, toothpaste and toothbrush, shampoo, and a potholder.

They would also receive a special treat: greeting cards, handmade and illustrated, from students at two Hawaii elementary schools. One card, on orange construction paper, started with a poem written by the class.

This isn't just a turkey, as anyone can see.
I made it with my hand which is a part of me.
It comes with a lot of love, especially to say
I hope you have a happy Thanksgiving Day.

The children added sweet personal notes. One card said, "Have a good dinner. Bless your heart."

I had brought my camera, intending to take pictures of the neighborhood, the house number, and each recipient. "Oh, no," Jackie said. "You can't do any of that. The names and addresses are confidential. These people are helpless."

While we were driving, a pleasant aroma of roast turkey wafted through the SUV. I learned something that Jackie and Leah already knew: delivery could be daunting. At one house we idled in front of a chain-link fence. There was no house number evident. We stood outside at the curb, puzzled. Jackie used her cell phone to call. The woman who answered said, "I don't need that. I don't want one." With gentle questioning, Jackie learned the woman thought she'd been disqualified from Meals on Wheels. Jackie persuaded her to accept our offerings.

These were a few of our other visits:

• A refrigerator stood outside the back door with a sign on it: "Please put Meals on Wheels in ice box." We did, including the sundries bag. We didn't get to see the recipient.

• A mustached elderly gentleman, solidly built but

moving slowly, said, "Thank you, thank you very much." And with tears in his eyes, "Thank you very very much." I got tears in my eyes, too.

• Up in the "Heights" of one neighborhood, a gentleman was outside watering his garden. The front door was open. We could see into the living room, where there was a large table covered with cages of young doves. One full-grown dove was flying around the ceiling. We could also see beyond the table, out his sliding glass doors—a stunning view of Honolulu harbor, the skyline, and the blue ocean.

• A small bent-over lady came to the door with her walker. She had a blue flowered tote bag hanging from one handle and tucked our offerings inside.

• A brisk lady with alert blue eyes was happy and grateful. She waved goodbye to us from her porch.

• Our last stop was at a clapboard house set far back from the street. The young woman thanked us for her father, who was standing outside watching us. She said, "He's weak and confused. He doesn't understand why you've come."

Our journey took two hours. At Jackie's house I picked up my car and left for home to make something-or-other for our family dinner. Jackie and Leah went into the house to cook. Our son-in-law Rodney was in the yard roasting two *char siu* turkeys on the Weber grill in preparation for fourteen Thanksgiving Day guests. It was another day to be grateful for my loving family, not just in Hawaii, but in eight states on the Mainland.

COVID-19 Calamity

As I wrote this in 2020, during the coronavirus pandemic, we all felt the impact of our Federal Government's lack of intelligent leadership. In 2018 President Trump disbanded the Federal pandemic preparation agency. Why on earth did he do that? Even decision-making by our Hawaii government was mired in quicksand. The perceptive journalist David Shapiro, in his *Honolulu Star-Advertiser* column a few months ago, said: "The state Health Department is in tatters....Never before has our public leadership been more fractured and ineffective."

So how are Larry and I personally coping? For two months our entire family here did the grocery shopping for us, as well as retrieving our many prescriptions. I finally discovered that Sam's Club and Long's had drive-up prescription pickups that I could easily handle, and I no longer had to depend on Jackie and Myrna. (It worried us plenty that we were subjecting them to crowds in stores.) Sam's Club can even mail prescriptions, which come by Fed Ex in a couple days. Most often, Larry and I order groceries delivered from Safeway.

Our condo of 136 units requires masks in all the common areas. In mid-August one of our residents tested positive for COVID. He was sent to a health-care facility and his family isolated themselves in their apartment.

I've been to Don Quijote (my "Donkey") only a few times. I go at 7:00 a.m. when few shoppers are there, and avoid those that are. I wear my mask and Latex gloves and take along a big piece of paper towel soaked with 409 cleaner. I vigorously wipe a cart down, handles, frame, the works, before taking it inside. The checkout line is often empty. If not, we stand six feet apart. But in December I discovered, to my dismay, that Donkey has discontinued its hot food deli. I miss it!

In mid-August Larry had outpatient surgery at Pali Momi Hospital in Aiea. I was allowed to stay with him until he was rolled to the operating room. Then I figured I'd pass the time at one of the pleasant outdoor tables in front of the cafeteria. No way. A security officer approached me and said nobody was allowed to sit in any of the normal waiting areas because of the COVID. "That's why there's nobody here or in the cafeteria. You can sit in your car if you want." The only other option was to leave and come back later.

Larry's surgery was only an hour. Fortunately, I had my word puzzles in the daily paper and a book. The doctor called me on my cell phone after surgery to tell me it went fine, Larry was in Recovery, and a nurse would let me know when I could come upstairs to be with him.

"I'm waiting in my car in the garage," I said.

The doctor's response: "That's pretty much the way it is everywhere now."

* * * *

Here in early 2021 the nightmare continues. On December 9th the daily number of cases in Hawaii was down to two digits. But, unhappily, that was yesterday. Today it's back up to three digits. The only good news is that a vaccine is now available. Still, I only rarely go to the supermarket and continue ordering groceries online. I look in my closet at all my lovely clothes and sigh. I have no place to wear them. And they're getting lonely!

Ironically, Hawaii was doing extremely well in the early stages. But then came the too-soon relaxation of rules: protest marches with hundreds of people crammed close together; stubborn socializing clusters; and all caution fell apart. What gets me most is those people who insist on their right *not* to wear a mask. Does that mean they're insisting on their right to get deathly ill? And to transmit their illness to others? Their demands defy all logic.

Truthfully, Larry and I wonder whether these scary, bizarre times will ever end. The toughest thing for me is not being able to hug and kiss my family! We may be seeing the light at the end of the tunnel. The vaccine has arrived here in Hawaii. As residents in the age group seventy-five and older, Larry and I have just received our first shot, with the second one scheduled for twenty-eight days later.

Chapter 3
LIFE WITH LARRY

"When I finally took her in my arms after a month of dating she wondered why I took so long."
—from Larry's autobiography, *No Place To Be But Here*

The Second Time Around - 37

The Second Time Around

Larry and I met on a blind date in October, 1986, at my house in Severna Park, Maryland. We came from rather different worlds. He had lost his wife to cancer. I'd been divorced for eight years, happily accustomed to having my own space, thank you.

Our dinner date was for six o'clock. I was ready at 5:45. I looked out the living room window and saw him sitting in his car reading a newspaper. He didn't want to come to the door early in case I wasn't ready. So considerate! Before we'd even met face to face, I was thinking, *This man is a keeper!*

In the car, on our way home from dinner, he said, "When I retire I'm going to write a novel and I want you to help me." Now neither of us had ever written fiction. I was an editor; he was an electrical engineer, and I'd only known this man for four hours. So I chirped, "Okay!" Again, instinct told me he was Mr. Right—and I'd better not let him get away.

That same night he slipped a pun into our dinner conversation. I parried with a small jab. "Do you pun in your sleep?"

"I think so," he said. "I was born in the Year of the Pun. That's the thirteenth sign of the Zaniac."

My psychoanalyst father loved Larry, but detested puns. Whenever he came to visit us and Larry tossed out another one, Father would groan, pull his plane ticket out of his breast pocket, and pretend to study it. "Yup, time to go back to Milwaukee."

After more than three decades of marriage to Larry, puns have osmosed their way into my psyche. And in telling you this I've just created a new verb.

Dating him I discovered he had another conversational habit: whimsically turning phrases around. I got so used to it that I started doing it, too. For a while, in a restaurant I worried I would tell our waiter: "I'll have the rot poast and pashed motatoes."

He also loved making plays on words. I asked: "What kind of sandwich are you ordering?"

"Threenafish." (Years later, I heard comedian Victor Borg

say the same thing in a whole series of skewed number-words. But Larry didn't get it from him; it was his own invention.)

Shortly after we were married, I discovered that my husband has an annoying super-smeller. Once, at midnight, I was downstairs in the kitchen snitching a few spoonfuls of peanut butter. I tiptoed into our large bedroom assuming Larry was asleep. I was wrong. Groggily, he asked, "Do I smell peanut butter?" I can't get away with anything.

Conversations:

Me: "I feel overwhelmed."

L: "You have to put clamps on your whelmer. Don't let it get over."

Me: "Goodwill is coming to pick up stuff."

L: "Great. I'll add my Goodwon't."

Me: "We'll make short shrift of that."

L: "What's a shrift?"

Me: "I don't know. I'll have to look it up. [I check the dictionary.] It's a confession."

L: "I didn't do it."

Me: "He's an upstanding person."

L: "Does that mean everyone else is downstanding?"

L: "Judges always holds hearings, never smellings."

Me: "I have to sew up that hole."

L: "Nobody sews anything down. They only sew it up."

Me at breakfast: "Dear, you've got a blob of strawberry jam on your T-shirt."

L: "Of course. My T-shirts need feeding three times a day to keep them alive."

Me at lunch: "Dear, you have a blob of blue cheese dressing

on your cheek."
L: "Doesn't everybody?"

I start coughing.
L: "You all right?"
Me: "I swallowed wrong."
L: "Bring it back up and try again. Get it right next time."

I pulled a hammer out of the tool drawer in Larry's desk. He asked, "Where are you going with that hammer?"

"I'm going to discipline the vacuum cleaner. It's stuck on High."

"Bring it here."

He turned it upside down, spun the wheels, and within five minutes had fixed it.

I asked, "If I had whacked it with the hammer would I have broken it?"

"For sure."

A few days after Larry and I retired, the full impact of it hit me. The Togetherness. After lunch, he was still sitting at the kitchen table and I was standing at the counter making Jell-O. Suddenly, I felt uncomfortable. "Larry, you're staring at me. Are you watching to see that I make the Jell-O correctly? Like I don't know how?"

"I'm an engineer. It's normal for me to check on how processes are going."

I bristled. "Really? Well! May *your* Jell-O never harden!"

He raised an eyebrow. "And may all *your* fruit sink to the bottom!"

I rushed in the door, up the stairs, and into our office. Larry was at his computer. In a burst of excitement I started telling him about my morning. As I was talking, telling the story in my slow, evolving way, a look of impatience crossed his face. He waved his arms and hands like he was scooping up handfuls of air.

"Get to the point," he said.

I was incensed. "What do you mean? I'm telling you the details first. I like to embellish and digress."

"But that's not how I process information," he said. "I have to be given the point first so I know which drawer to file it in—in my head."

I stared at him in disbelief. I was contending with mental filing cabinets? "But that's rude," I insisted. "I want to tell the story my way, and it's a free country. It's my privilege to tell it my way."

"Yes," he retorted, "but then I will miss the point."

"I bet you wouldn't behave this way if I were a friend telling you something."

"Probably not. But…" and he smiled, "I'd probably just dismiss it altogether."

I sighed and shook my head. There was no winning this one. My engineer husband had to process information his way. But it sure took the fun out of telling him a story. Funny, how I never noticed this about him when we were both working in the defense industry, nine-hour days or longer. Maybe we just didn't have time for these intricate exchanges. Or…I was busy sifting through my own mental file folders to give him my whole day in ten minutes.

I use those large pastel-colored kitchen sponges. They're really good, but once they get dirty there's no cleaning them. In desperation I doused one in bleach. Instantly, the sponge turned pristine clean. But two days later, I was standing at the sink watching it totally disintegrate.

"Larry, what's happening? The bleach worked so well."

"How much water did you mix with the bleach?"

"Water?"

I've told Larry more than once that he has to outlive me. He scowls. He doesn't find that the least bit funny. I do. He possesses technical skills even in his sleep. If I outlive him, here's what I will not be able to do at our apartment.

• Unsnag problems while operating any of our computers or load new software.

• Put new toner in our black-and-white and color printers.

• Manipulate all our TV remotes. The master for TV, the one for Netflix and Prime, the one for the DVD player; and who knows what else.

• Enter all our financial data down to the last penny on a spreadsheet each month. When it's early in a new year, there are three activities I'm responsible for so he can do our taxes: the spreadsheets for our charity gifts; our interminable list of prescriptions; and the annual sales log for our books. Only a few days ago he taught me how to delete last year's data to start fresh—by sitting at my computer and showing me step by step as I wrote each step down on a legal pad. (I had never before asked him to walk me through the process so precisely.) However, no way can I ever manage the formula to fix a glitch in one of the spreadsheets. Such complexities were invented by Microsoft techies to shut out the rest of us and make themselves feel needed.

Larry's a good storyteller. He's often told me anecdotes about his Navy career during the Korean War or growing up in New Haven, Connecticut, and I was always spellbound. I noticed that when he told these little stories to our friends, they were virtually on the edge of their chairs. So for ten years I begged him to write his memoirs. Or at least short essays. In 2018 he took my advice. But my husband never does anything halfway. He started with the day of his birth and wrote his autobiography—448 pages, and published it in 2019: *No Place To Be But Here: My Life and Times*. It's a wise and absorbing book.

Chapter 4
MY SENIOR DECADE

"Getting old is not for sissies."—**Bette Davis**

"The biggest lie I tell myself is 'I don't need to write it down, I'll remember it.'"—**Aunty Acid,** *Quirky Quotes*

Other people have senior moments, I'm
having a Senior Decade. Several, in fact.

Larry got out the little tub of margarine for lunch, opened it, and discovered a coffee filter filled with used coffee grounds. It was garbage I'd prepared to throw away. At breakfast I'd been rushing to get ready for my Jazzercise class and I put it in the fridge instead. Does that mean I threw away the actual tub of margarine? Mercifully, I've forgotten.

I set the automatic coffeepot for 7:00 a.m. I placed the grounds in the filter basket and slid the glass carafe full of water carefully in its place—instead of pouring the water inside the top of the coffeemaker. Next morning, entering the kitchen, Larry said, "I smell something burning." I sniffed. "It's the coffeepot!" I yelled. He quickly unplugged it—just before it burned out the appliance's elements.

I know I'm a fairly smart person. So why do I keep doing dumb things? This is the latest and worst one yet. April, 2020—stuck at home under the COVID-19 lockdown. Mail comes, a letter for Larry and one for me, from the same address. It's an announcement. "The Writers Conference sponsored by the National League of American Pen Women, scheduled for June, has been canceled. Enclosed is your refund check." We had enrolled early.

Mindlessly, dementedly, instead of reading the letter and studying the checks carefully, I assumed they were my own checks. I got out a magic marker and wrote VOID in black letters on each one. A week later, looking through my checkbook, I realized I had not written checks for the conference. I had paid for them online with a credit card. It took me a week to get up the *chutzpah* to write a letter to the NLAPW co-president who signed the checks. I enclosed them, apologized to high heaven, and begged her to send me new checks.

A few days later, with her typical grace and kindness, she reissued our checks.

Our kids were coming for dinner. They called us from the front door on the condo intercom, and I tried to buzz them in. Nothing happened. I asked Larry, "What's wrong?" He laughed. "You're using the TV remote instead of punching number nine on the phone."

Unable to sleep, at 2:00 a.m. I shuffled into the kitchen for a few sips of diet tonic water, hoping it would relax me. No need to put on my glasses. I saw a creepy crawly cockroach high up on the cabinet over the fridge. After fumbling under the sink for the can of Raid, I sprayed the invader good and hard and long. Next morning I strolled into the kitchen for breakfast. Now that I had my glasses on, I discovered that I had sprayed an exposed, unpainted cabinet screw.

At Safeway checkout, I took my two enormous packs of toilet paper off the belt and stowed them efficiently in my cart—before having them scanned! I was lucky the checkout clerk didn't call Security.

During the COVID-19 lockdown, I went online to Safeway's delivery service and found it easy to choose what I wanted from the pictures shown. Then I went to Roma tomatoes, Larry's daily favorites. I clicked on "2." When the bags were delivered, everything I ordered was there—except for the tomatoes. In a tiny baggie sat two puny Romas. If I had noticed the price next to the picture, $1.60, I would have realized I was paying for two tomatoes, not two pounds.

In 2003 we were driving Emily, our five-year-old granddaughter, to a roller skating birthday party at the Hippodrome in Augusta, Georgia. *Ah,* I thought, *a chance to try in-line skates.* The man behind the counter scowled. "You don't want those. They're for racing, they have no brakes." He handed me a pair of four-wheelers. I spent the next half-hour churning round and round the vast indoor rink just trying to keep my balance. The skates were so clunky.

The birthday girl's dad came gliding up beside me, the friendly host. Maybe the spinning strobes had taken a few decades off my face, casting their romantic droplets of light like snowflakes.

"How long has it been since you roller-skated?" the dad asked.

His question caught me off guard. I had to count back to 1948 when I was thirteen. In my Milwaukee suburb of Whitefish Bay, we strapped on ball-bearing skates and tightened them with a square key. Finally, I reported: "Fifty-five years."

"Oh," he said, and skated away.

I'm so well organized that I have a red folder on my desk labeled URGENT BUSINESS. The problem is, some of the stuff in it is from 2015.

Larry's scalp ointment that I put on him every night disappeared off his night table. I searched the apartment like a crazy person, including his sock drawers and the medicine chest. The next day I found it in my medications drawer, buried under the Aspercreme. Hours later I realized why. It was supposed to be buried there. The day before, the dermatologist had switched him to something else and given us samples and a new prescription.

A few weeks ago I came home from Donkey shopping and told Larry, "I'm missing one bag." I had put all the groceries away. My wire cart was empty and I knew I'd also bought cream cheese, margarine, and boxed soups. But where was the bag? Had I left it on the counter at Donkey? I leaped to the kitchen phone and called Customer Service. The lady said she'd ask the checkout person at that counter. I could hear much noise in the background; customers and business going on at an Indy-500 pace. And I was disrupting them! After five minutes, the Customer Service lady came back and politely informed me, "No bag was left on the counter." I thanked her and hung up. Taking a shame-faced breath, I decided to sit down at the table and try to figure this thing out. Which is what I should have done in the first place. I'd bought too much to fit in my own cart; I had to carry one bag. When I got to our apartment door, I had set it down on the hall floor to get my key out.

Oh, dear. I jumped up from the table, opened the apartment door, and there sat my missing bag, just where I'd left it.

Woody Allen's play title *You Know I Can't Hear You When the Water's Running* is sheer brilliance. I'm always saying it to Larry. Ah, yes, how many times a day have we misunderstood each other. Our condo multiplies the chances because it's a wonderful older building with concrete walls. We do a lot of grousing, especially if we're in different rooms: "What did you say?"

Recently, I heard—yes, heard—the perfect example of dwindling hearing ability at a Zoom meeting during COVID-19. (It applies to Larry and me all too often.) Before the meeting started, we were all chatting via Zoom. "Bill" mentioned one of his favorite authors, and asked the rest of us what books we were reading. He addressed "Howard," a ninety-year-old who had joined the meeting while eating his breakfast.

"Howard? What are *you* reading?"

"Oatmeal."

Our Jewish Wisdom class normally met every Tuesday morning in the Temple Emanu-El library, led by Rabbi Ken Aronowitz. Before COVID, that is. During COVID it's Zoomed.

A couple years ago we often brought our friend Celia with us. She was ninety-six and used a walker, which we'd stow in our Honda trunk. On this particular morning, other friends in the class, Diane and her husband (another) Larry, suggested that the five of us go out to lunch at Dave and Buster's downtown.

"Fine," we said. After class I tucked Celia into our back seat and fastened her seatbelt-harness. Efficiently, breezily, I jumped into the driver's seat and off we went. When we arrived at Dave and Buster's I opened our trunk to get the walker out. It wasn't there! I had left it in the temple parking lot! Celia couldn't walk without it. I made a quick call to Stephanie, the temple administrator, to bring the walker into the office, turned the car around, and took us back to temple to retrieve it. Of course, Diane and Larry were wondering what had happened to us. Fortunately, they took a booth and waited patiently until we finally arrived for lunch—with my embarrassed explanation.

Sometimes being super-efficient just doesn't work.

Chapter 5
A MEDLEY OF REFLECTIONS

"Sometimes what you need is already there."
—Song from the film *The Life Ahead*

My Helpful Brain

It never ceases to amaze me. I'm going crazy looking for something in our apartment, like my super-size flashlight. I give up in exasperation, have supper, watch TV. Suddenly, I spring up from my recliner and beeline straight to the shelf where I'd randomly left it. The reason I find it? Even though I'd stopped looking, my brain kept working for me. It also happens often when I'm doing a crossword puzzle. Larry and I work them together at the kitchen table or separately when we each have a few spare minutes. I ask myself, *Why can't I think of this word? I should know it.* Later I sit down again, study the puzzle, and remember the word. Again, my brain chooses to joyfully keep working on my behalf. It's a miracle. (Now if it would only remind me immediately that there's nothing wrong with our car's air conditioning. I've got it set on Heat!)

Am I a member of The Bad Luck Club? No matter which performance I attend: our opera season, Diamond Head Theatre, even a movie, the largest, tallest people on the planet are sitting smack in front of me. The towering lady with emerald-green hair matching her emerald-green dress. The man with head, shoulders, and neck the size of Delaware. It's a conspiracy. The theater gods are against me. At least they were until COVID came along. Once we're able to attend again, I'll most likely be in the same fix.

In front of Aina Haina Library, waiting for it to open, a man sat on a bench holding the leash of his handsome German shepherd. I decided to commune with it. "What a lovely dog you are," I cooed, and he responded, Whooooo! in a prolonged dog-soprano voice.

My pet peeve in restaurants is an overzealous waiter asking me.

"Are you still working on that?"

"No," I'm tempted to snap. "I'm eating." I'm quite sure he's about to pull the fork out of my mouth.

At our house in Severna Park, the single step from our front door to the porch was steeper than it used to be, because the cement porch had settled over the years. For the first time, some friends in their seventies had trouble navigating it. One friend had Parkinson's, another was a cancer survivor, and a third one had a stroke five days after visiting us. I'm pretty sure our step wasn't to blame.

$Everything$ I learn these days seems to come from either *Reader's Digest* or crossword puzzles. Headlight gas is xenon! Somehow I haven't found a way to work that into cocktail party conversation.

We were in the waiting room of our doctor's office in Annapolis, and in walked Marty and Sheila Litzky. With her incomparable insight, Sheila said, "You know you're getting older when you meet your friends of forty years in the urologist's office."

My thirty-year-old vacuum cleaner wheezes and whines, like it feels put-upon when it's required to perform. It seems to be having its own Senior Decade.

Speaking of vacuum cleaners...A friend in Severna Park once told me a pesky neighbor was always coming over to visit without calling or warning, always about the same time (and always overstaying). Kathy devised the perfect solution. She wheeled the vacuum cleaner into the living room and looked out the window. As the neighbor approached, Kathy turned on the vac, set it near the front door, and went upstairs. The neighbor realized Kathy couldn't hear the doorbell with the vac running, so she'd turn around and go home.

"Smithies" Take a Stand

I'm a Smith College graduate, class of 1957. Our marvelous class secretary, Judy Snow Denison, has developed a special email forum for us. In November, 2020 we discussed a post-election crisis. A Smith alumna (class of '95), Emily W. Murphy, was the administrator of the U.S. Government Services Administration. A Trump appointee, she refused to recognize Joe Biden as the president-elect. Her refusal meant withholding the critical GSA funding needed to run the U.S. Government. Under Judy's direction, we sent Emily Murphy the following Open Letter—signed by eighty-nine Smithies!

We are writing to you today as fellow Smith College alumnae.

As the GSA Administrator, you have a significant responsibility in this moment: to sign the document that releases the government support after the presidential election for the smooth transition between administrations of the US government. The "apparent winner" must receive the go-ahead so that the transition can move forward. There is a national danger to our democracy in the delay that the GSA is causing....Please act on your obligation to protect the transition. You have a role in this threat to our democratic election process. Your denial will cause more COVID-19 deaths and delay delivery of the vaccine....

This is so sad. You have had an exquisite education that has given you the capacity for critical thinking and you are squandering it. Think again, study the facts and include the writing of history. What do you want your reputation to become? You still have a chance to redeem it. Please hear the voice of history—for the president, for truth and for you.

It is our obligation, as citizens and as Smith alumnae, to address this issue basic to our democracy and security. It is our obligation to "speak Truth to Power."

Emily received a similar nationwide petition (from the general public) containing over 240,000 signatures. A few days after our letter was received, Emily released the GSA funds. We have no idea whether our class letter made any difference, but I felt proud that we did not sit back in silence.

Horsing Around

On the phone with our daughter Myrna I complained, "I'm on my way to Dementia Country. Maybe you should start looking for a nice pasture to put me out in." (I say that a lot these days.)

Myrna: "Would you like a horse to go with that?"

At the time the Spurriers were living on their horse farm in South Carolina. I happen to adore horses—to look at them, pet them, feed them a palmful of grass, but not to be on them. You see, I have this horse history. When I was eight, at Camp Willowbank, I fell off a horse. Not his fault. He was quietly standing still with the other horses and us kids sitting on them. But I fell off anyway and extended my left arm to break my fall. What I did break was my wrist—a nasty compound fracture. Next thing I knew I was hustled into the back of a camp official's car, wrapped in blankets, and driven back home to Milwaukee, an hour away.

Two years later, my mother sent me to Joy Farm Day Camp. Riding was part of our daily routine, in an indoor rink with a counselor riding next to each of us. No way could a camper fall off a horse. But I hated it. The trauma of Camp Willowbank haunted me. When I got home the afternoon of the first day, Mother asked me: "How was it?"

"We rode horses and I fell off five times." I hadn't decided in advance to lie. Subconsciously, I must have assumed Mother would cancel camp and let me stay home. She didn't. Instead, she called the director to complain. The next day, the counselor assigned to ride next to me sneered, "You fell off five times." Don't ask me why I lied to my mother. I did it many times and it was always a bad idea. Curiously, she didn't confront me and try to get to the bottom of it.

That wasn't my last time on a horse. Freshman year at Smith College we had to take Physical Education. I chose horseback riding for first semester, hoping I'd get over my fears. The instructor taught us to trot and canter, but when she watched me, all she ever said was, "Oh that poor horse!" She never tried to correct me. I somehow got through the class and so did my poor horses. And believe it or not, Smith actually wrote my parents asking them to help fund a new riding rink. The *chutzpah*! Second semester I gratefully turned to fencing.

We visited the Spurriers at their horse farm every summer, a ten-hour drive from Severna Park. On our last visit, Ben had a special chore: to clean the horses' hooves. Now, he could have hired a farrier to do it, but it was expensive. He brought out Fannie from the field where she was grazing with her pals, and sat down on a low stool to perform hoof-cleaning. Being rather new at this, it took him almost fifteen minutes for each hoof. I volunteered to help, which meant standing in front of Fannie, stroking her, talking to her, and diverting her attention from spending almost an hour on three legs. She rewarded me with a huge, sloppy lick on my mouth. Kissed by a horse. What a treat!

Laundry 101

Doing laundry used to be so easy. All the whites went in one load and all the colored stuff in the second load. Job done. Now it's a ritual, a science, a pain in the neck. At least now I try to read the instructions. Several years ago, I tossed a pair of rayon pants in and turned the usual dial to Warm/Warm. I had assumed that rayon meant a tough, versatile fabric because it was a synthetic with an "o-n" ending. Wrong! The pants not only shrank, they also shriveled up. Sixty dollars down the drain. I told my sad story to my Korean alterations lady. "Rayon!" she scoffed. "I no buy."

So here I am, ready to wash my pile of tops. Just tops, nothing else. The instruction labels go like this:

- Fuchsia cotton shirt: *Machine wash cold, gentle cycle.*
- Navy rayon/nylon: *Dry clean only.*
- Blue viscose/nylon: *Machine wash cold, lay flat to dry.* (Viscose? Is that a new endangered species?)
- Black and white striped cotton: *Machine wash warm, like colors, tumble dry low.* (Will someone please tell me how you put a black and white garment in with "like" colors?)
- Two crinkly polyester/cotton blouses: *Machine wash cold, squeeze in towel, no dryer.*
- Sparkly top with sequins and beads: *Turn inside out, hand wash cold, lay flat to dry.*
- Cotton shirt I bought in Israel: Never mind, the instructions are in Hebrew.
- Plus one innocent little Nike workout shirt, polyester/spandex/nylon, with these eight commands:
  o *Machine wash cold with like colors.*
  o *Do not use softeners.*
  o *Remove immediately.*
  o *Do not bleach.*
  o *Line dry.*
  o *Do not iron.*
  o *Do not dry clean.*
  o *Do not allow to lay on itself when wet. (What exactly does "lay on itself" mean? Curl up in a fetal position? Double over in pain? And shouldn't it be "lie" instead of "lay?")*

Maybe it's time for colleges to add a new course to their curriculum: Laundry 101.

The Hardest Thing

The hardest thing about being in our eighties is the inevitable reality: our family members and friends who have died. When we reminisce about them, saying their names, do we have to add "of blessed memory"? We feel it deeply, but it sounds so stilted. I figure they know. They know we're talking about them, remembering them at their most loving and fun, so they excuse us.

I'm thinking right now of our friends Marty Kogan and his wife, Bobbi (and here I go again, of blessed memory). We went to China together in 2001. Marty once got philosophical in our conversation. "I believe we're born with a certain number of heartbeats. We have to take it slowwwwww," he said in a deep, mellow voice, "so we don't use them up before our time."

Manny (of blessed memory) and Go Nodar were our cousins in Roswell, Georgia, a northwest suburb of Atlanta. Go is still thriving. Manny lives on in so many ways. His wit was memorable. The first time we visited them, he said: "When we go out, one drives, the other screams."

During that same visit, Larry and I stayed at a Holiday Inn Express. Our third morning, we arrived at the Nodars' for breakfast with me in a surly mood.

"You know what that idiot maid did cleaning our room yesterday? She threw out our bottle of Metamucil on the dresser and the paper cup and plastic spoon with it. She assumed they were garbage." (The Metamucil was for Larry to take with his nighttime pills. I had to mix it with water even when we traveled.)

Manny calmed me down. "I have the perfect solution for you: fiber pills. I get 'em at Sam's Club." Fiber pills? That was news to us. We're also members of Sam's. He drove us right over, marched us into the Pharmacy aisles, straight to the double-bottled package of fiber pills. To this day, we thank Manny for delivering us from Metamucil.

During that same visit, Cousin Go took us on a little tour of Roswell and we ended up at a park. Sitting at a waterside picnic table, Go said, "That's the Chattahoochee River." Wow! I had only heard of it vaguely as somewhere in the South. And here we were. Years later, on another visit, Go took our daughter Jackie and me to the Chattahoochee Nature Center. As we were leaving, I came upon a sign: "The Okefenokee Swamp." Wow again! The largest freshwater swamp in the world, straddling Georgia and Florida, half a million acres. Back at the house, I told Larry about it and showed him my iPhone picture of the sign.

"That's where Pogo lived," he said.

Pogo was one of my mother's absolute favorite comic strips. She was a journalist and book author and still loved the comics.

Mother died when I was twenty-one. I'm missing her still.

Chapter 6
CLOSE ENCOUNTERS OF THE FLEETING KIND

"There is not one big cosmic meaning for all, there is only the meaning we each give to life…To give as much meaning to one's life as possible is right to me."

*—The Diary of **Anais Nin***

Arthur Ochs Sulzberger

The summer between my junior and senior years at Whitefish Bay High School in Milwaukee, I got a job as a copy girl (a glorified gofer) in the City Room at the *Milwaukee Journal,* an evening paper with a stellar national reputation. My mother got me the job; she was a frequent feature writer for the *Journal.*

Such a thrill. Every week I had a crush on a different reporter. My shift began at 6:30 a.m. and one of my jobs was to clip out significant articles in the morning *Sentinel* so the reporters could pursue expanded stories for the *Journal.* Clipping the articles meant tearing them out using a ruler, not a scissors. My boss for this assignment was the managing editor, a stern man and a perfectionist. My second morning he handed me another copy of the *Sentinel* and said, "Do the clippings over. The edges are fuzzy. Be more precise."

One day somebody new was occupying a City Room desk: Arthur Ochs "Punch" Sulzberger. His father was publisher of the *New York Times* and he was in line to inherit the post. He was at the *Journal* for about a year of hands-on experience. He was a handsome man with dark eyes and dark hair, and he smoked a pipe, which sat firmly in his square jaw. Frequently, I heard sharp words floating from his desk. Yup. The managing editor, unhappy with some aspects of his stories. But he sat there unflappable, perhaps because he'd served as a Marine in World War II. Mother invited him and his wife to our house for dinner. They accepted, but it was a rather stilted evening. Still, I admired Mother for her gesture.

Arthur Ochs Sulzberger became publisher of the *New York Times* in 1963. It won sixty Pulitzer Prizes under his nearly thirty years of leadership, notably for David Halberstam's Vietnam dispatches and *The Pentagon Papers.*

Marchesa Cecilia Zimmerman Barbaro St. George

The Marchesa Cecilia Zimmerman Barbaro St. George had recently married Dr. John F. Pick, a professor of English at Marquette University in Milwaukee—and a friend of my parents. Here again was Mother pulling strings to make my life more exciting. I was spending my junior year with the Smith College Group in Geneva, Switzerland.

Cecilia lived in Valletta, capital of Malta, an island sixty miles south of Sicily and part of the British Commonwealth. She was a member of one of Malta's oldest and most distinguished royal families. During our spring break at the University of Geneva, four of us classmates went to Italy. Mother arranged for me to fly from Rome to Valletta to visit the marchesa, who had graciously invited me to spend several days.

I think "Cissy" was her nickname, but I'm not sure, so I'll refrain from calling her that. Cecilia's stately villa had foot-thick concrete walls and no heat. In 1956 all of Europe was experiencing its coldest winter in a quarter-century. When I washed my stockings and hung them up to dry, three days later they were still icy-damp.

At breakfast my first morning I discovered a whole solitary orange sitting on my plate. Nothing else. I was accustomed to making orange juice with our little hand squeezer at home, but I had never actually peeled an orange and soon found myself with pulp and juice all the way up to my wrists. This was no way to make a good impression on royalty. Cecilia came to my rescue by peeling the mangled orange for me.

That was only part of my awkwardness. I had already gained ten pounds in Europe from all the pasta and pastry, and most often I had to wear my gray plaid wool suit because it was one of the few things that still fit. It had an A-line skirt that made the bottom half of me look like a triangle.

The marchesa had an elegant demeanor, served sherry to her English friends every afternoon, and kindly introduced me to several young men. One took me dancing. Another one took me to meet his friends on their houseboat: two Egyptian naval officers and the daughter of a renowned American doctor. My third date was a dashing guy who kissed me goodnight quite passionately at the bottom of Cecilia's sweeping staircase. Suddenly, I heard her commanding voice. "Rosemary, get upstairs this minute!" Turns out he was engaged; nobody had told me.

Four months after my visit, Cecilia and John boarded the Italian luxury liner *Andrea Doria,* on their way to the U.S. to settle in Milwaukee. On the last leg of the voyage, near Nantucket, disaster struck. On July 25, 1956, a Swedish ship rammed into the hull; the captain had misread his radar and thought the *Andria Dorea* was still a mile away. Among the 1,200-plus passengers, forty-six died. The ship sank the next day. Mercifully, Cecilia and John survived.

Pat Nixon

In the late 1960s, during the first Nixon Administration, Pat Nixon invited me to tea at the White House. Oh, not me personally. I just happened to be in the right place at the right time. I was a Smith alumna and received the invitation as a member of the Smith College Club of Washington. This special event had been generously arranged by Julie Nixon Eisenhower, also a Smith alumna.

My first husband and I were living in College Park, Maryland, only forty-five minutes from the White House. The invitation read: "The first 250 to respond will be included." Within minutes of receiving it, I rushed to the post office with my acceptance.

I had not voted for Nixon. I was an impassioned Democrat, but this was an irresistible opportunity. So irresistible that I left my daughter, Miriam, only eighteen months old and suffering from a nasty cold, with a babysitter.

At the proper gate, with all of us assembled, Security checked our invitations. In hushed anticipation, we filed into a great hall. Bronze Remington statues with their Western themes graced side tables. We were ushered up the red-carpeted staircase to the East Room.

Before I even spotted Mrs. Nixon, I discovered that we were surrounded by an exhibit of Andrew Wyeth original paintings. In one corner, a chamber orchestra played exquisitely. Tuxedoed waiters floated about with silver trays, offering us tea and glasses of drinks, as well as delicate hors d'oeuvres and tiny pastries. I felt myself glowing with good fortune.

The First Lady sat demurely in a chair along one wall. She struck me as poised, unassuming, and gracious. The woman in charge of Protocol arranged us in a receiving line and instructed us to state our names. My turn came. "Rosemary Wolfe," I said. That was my name in my first marriage. Mrs. Nixon smiled and replied: "That's the name of my husband's secretary."

I smiled back and thought, *How charming of her to respond in such a personal way*. Years later, during the Watergate scandal in the early '70s, I recalled my afternoon at the White House with Pat Nixon. And it suddenly occurred to me why she'd responded to my name the way she did. I had spoken it too softly. Mrs. Nixon thought I introduced myself as "Rose Mary Woods"—the name of President Nixon's devoted secretary, who allegedly, accidentally, deleted about four minutes of the notorious eighteen minutes of tape.

At that moment I felt a pang of sadness for Mrs. Nixon. Such a lovely person, and what a terrible ordeal she was enduring.

James Watson

My first job after graduation was as an advertising copywriter at Allyn & Bacon, a textbook publisher on Beacon Hill in Boston. My roommate and I lived three blocks away, on Myrtle Street in a tiny $95-a-month apartment.

I had a scholarly friend from Milwaukee, Richard, who was a classics major at Harvard. When we went out for supper he'd tell me wonderful things he'd just learned, like: "You know the quote 'And another soldier bites the dust.' That sounds so modern, but it's actually from *The Iliad.*"

Once Richard invited me to a Harvard cocktail party. He drifted away to schmooze and left me standing alone, when a young man came up to me and introduced himself: "James Watson."

Oh my God! I knew the name. Everyone did. In 1953 he and Francis Crick discovered the structure of DNA, a double helix, which revealed how genetic material is passed on from generation to generation. I tried to make conversation, but what do you say to the man who has discovered the secret of life? *Oh, Dr. Watson, I looooove your double helix!* I don't think so.

He walked away.

J. H. Van Vleck

After a year at Allyn & Bacon, in 1958 I yearned to work at Harvard, but the only job opening was as a secretary in the Department of Physics. I took it. Big mistake. I was plunked down in the department library as the secretary to Professor J.H. Van Vleck. He was a famous physicist who had established the fundamentals of the quantum mechanical theory of magnetism (and a lot of other stuff I don't understand). I realized I'd be taking dictation, so I took a quick night course in Speed Writing. Professor Van Vleck was a small man with a deeply lined face and gravelly voice. He barked his dictation with great speed. But within minutes I discovered that I was miles out of my depth. I had absolutely no knowledge of physics terminology. The very next day, I was transferred to the department office in charge of graduate students' records.

If I had known Professor Van Vleck's credentials, I would have fainted on the spot and required smelling salts. In 1942, J. Robert Oppenheimer invited him and seven other theoretical physicists to participate in the Manhattan Project. Within three months they developed the principles of atomic bomb design. Prof. Van Vleck's work led to the establishment of the Los Alamos Nuclear Weapons Laboratory. He was a member of the Los Alamos Review committee. Its major contribution was a reduction in the size of the firing gun for the Little Boy bomb, eventually released over Hiroshima.

One day I discovered that Professor Van Vleck was also an art film buff. He came into the office on business, then stood in the center of the floor looking off into space, and asked me and the other secretary: "Have either of you seen *Wild Strawberries?* Neither of us had. A couple years later I did see it, an Ingmar Bergmann film of an aging professor reflecting on his life.

In 1977 J.H. Van Vleck shared the Nobel Prize in Physics.

It took me six months to realize that the heady atmosphere of the Harvard Department of Physics was doing nothing for my own future. I was merely a tool for the brilliant faculty members to further their careers. I spent most of my days doing grunt work. On purple-backed mimeograph paper, with my manual typewriter I typed the graduate students' tests and exams; they were studded with formulas, including subscripts and superscripts. A typo was inconceivable. Whenever I made one, I had to scratch it out with a razor blade. There were occasional moments of pride. I typed one letter (when his personal secretary was away) for Edward Purcell, 1952 Nobel Prizewinner for magnetic resonance imaging. Once I took dictation (and got it right!) for Norman F. Ramsey: his report as the Science Advisor to NATO. And I did some work for physicist Gerald Holton, who is still, at age 98, a great humanist. He retired as a physics professor and Professor of the History of Science, Emeritus at Harvard. Among his many books, he coauthored *Physics, the Human Adventure: From Copernicus to Einstein and Beyond,* a landmark in science education.

After a year in the department, in 1959, I was ready to move to New York to go into publishing and share an apartment with my actress cousin. The week before I left, the graduate students gave me a going-away party and a beautiful beaded necklace. Professor Holton gave me a lovely book, a biography of Marcel Proust.

In New York I went to work for *Harper's Magazine.* I started as a secretary, edited the Letters to the Editor column, and two years later, got promoted to assistant editor.

David Halberstam

A huge shadow blanketed my desk and typewriter. Startled, I looked up. A tall, mysterious-looking man towered in the doorway. This looming stranger struck me as intensely male, over six feet tall, with unorthodox good looks. Not handsome, but rugged, powerful, with big shoulders, lanky legs, a longish face with a quite heavy, although shaven, beard. He studied me from behind horn-rimmed glasses with piercing dark eyes borne of experience and wisdom and intellect. I inhaled his virility and brains.

Standing behind him was my editor-in-chief, Jack Fischer. "Rosemary, this is David Halberstam." And to David, "Rosemary is one of our assistant editors." David nodded and sat down at the only other desk in my cramped, windowless office.

"Hello," he said in a mellow bass voice.

"Hi." I didn't actually say "Hi" like a normal person. No, I squeaked it or whispered it. My civilized voice failed me, my throat closed up. I felt like I was strangling.

This was THE David Halberstam: the *New York Times* foreign correspondent who had reported the real story about Vietnam in 1962 and 1963. The David Halberstam whose dispatches from Saigon revealed how the United States had embroiled itself in a hideous, unwinnable war. President John F. Kennedy had summoned the publisher of the *New York Times*, Arthur Ochs Sulzburger, to the White House and leaned on him to remove David from his Southeast Asia beat. Sulzburger refused. In 1964, David won the Pulitzer Prize for these dispatches.

He left the *New York Times* to join *Harper's* as a contributing editor. This desk, normally occupied by another assistant editor, just happened to be free. For five days in June, 1967, I shared my space at 2 Park Avenue with David Halberstam.

I was so much in awe of him that I lived out the week tongue-tied, in terrified silence. Which didn't make sense in the least, because he was totally unpretentious and approachable.

Today, in my richly woven fantasy, I can imagine him feeling a rude culture shock. Here he was, back in New York—from Africa, where he'd been hit by shrapnel while in the Congo; from Vietnam, where he'd slogged through the jungle with our troops; and from Poland, whose government expelled him for his blunt reporting. Here he was, plunked down in my barren cubicle with its thin tweed carpet, metal desks, and walls the tannish-mustard color of newborn baby poop. A tornado of opportunities to talk to him swirled and funneled around me. But during that week, I burrowed into the basement of my mind. I might just as well have crawled under my desk, into the dark, safe space where I normally dangled my feet.

So how come? Well, it's like this. Erica Jong had her fear of flying and her fear of reaching fifty. I have my fear of authority figures. Whether they're fearsome or not. Whether they're actually in authority over me or not. That particular week, I was thirty-two years old, a grownup, and David was actually only two years older than I. But his presence in my office—and so physically imposing to boot—threw me into a state of mute terror. The diplomatic Mr. Halberstam never let on; he just acted pleasant and gracious, as if it were perfectly normal to be ignored this way.

David moved out of my office a week later, when my colleague returned to reclaim her desk. Shortly after, I left *Harper's* to follow my first husband to College Park, Maryland, and his new job. Perhaps it's just as well that I left. I already hero-worshipped David. Just a few more days and I'd have fallen crazy in love with him. So why am I telling this story five decades later? Because of his untimely death at age seventy-three as a passenger in a car accident on April 23, 2007. And why I personally feel such a monstrous sense of loss.

David's *Harper's* articles drew blistering portrayals of the Kennedy-Johnson Administration officials and laid the groundwork for his book *The Best and the Brightest*. The 700-page tome is an important historical document on how our foreign policy led up to the Vietnam debacle.

Here's a typical quote from *The Best and the Brightest:*

"The key to Lyndon Johnson was the capacity to move men to his objective and away from their own charted course.... Since he was not a contemplative man, a man who read books, and since he had little belief in the rhythms and thrusts of history, he was convinced that you could accomplish things by reasoning with leaders, by moving them to your goal, manipulating them a little, and that finally, all men had a price. In part, this helped bring him into trouble in Vietnam, with his instinct to personalize. He and Ho Chi Minh out there alone, in a shoot-out. He would find Ho's price, Ho's weakness, whether it was through bombing the North or through threatening to use troops, and then offering Ho a lollipop, massive economic aid...This time he would find himself dealing with a man who was a true revolutionary, incorruptible, a man who had no price, or at least no price that Lyndon Johnson with his Western bombs and Western dollars could meet. But it would take him quite a while to find out that he had met his match."

David was a compelling storyteller. His eight books provide gripping analyses of American politics, economics, entertainment, and sports, including *Playing for Keeps: Michael Jordan and the World He Made.* One of my favorite descriptions is his insight into the young, unknown Elvis Presley in *The Fifties.*

"He had been sent there by a talent scout who had not wanted anything to do with him—those awful pegged pants, the pink and black clothes. He was an odd mixture of a hood—the haircut, the clothes, the sullen, alienated look; and a sweet little boy—curiously gentle and respectful…Everyone was sir or ma'am. Few young Americans, before or after, have looked so rebellious and been so polite."

Henry Kissinger

A t *Harper's Magazine*, my desk was just inside the front door and my telephone sat on the back left corner of the desk. One morning (sometime in 1965), Henry Kissinger was visiting our editor-in-chief, discussing a potential article for the magazine. From 1955 to 1968 Kissinger was a key adviser on security issues to three presidents: Eisenhower, Kennedy, and Johnson.

After his appointment with Jack Fischer, he was on his way out, but stopped at my desk. Picking up my phone receiver he dialed his office. I assumed he was calling his secretary. With a glimmer of amusement on his face, he said, "I'm on my way in. Look busy."

In 1973 Henry Kissinger became President Nixon's Secretary of State.

Michi Naruo

W hen Larry and I decided to retire in 1993, we thought that four winter months in Honolulu, where our daughter Jackie and son-in-law Rodney live, would be plenty. After our first trip, on returning home in March, we paid the taxi driver and stumbled with our luggage into the kitchen, eager for a look into our back-

yard. What we saw was thick snow on the yellow forsythia blossoms. Hey, that was not good. We decided then and there, four
months in Honolulu was too short. From now on, six months!

Then it was a matter of finding an apartment. On our next
trip, we got word of one in a high-rise condo in the heart of Honolulu. We made an appointment to meet with the Japanese landlady
in apartment 403 that afternoon. She was visiting and conducting
business here from her home in California.

Michi Naruo was in her seventies, with silver-gray hair,
large rimless glasses, and a warm, sincere smile. Her adult daughter
Kathy Reed had accompanied her. We sat in the sunny living room,
filled them in on who we were, and eagerly asked Michi if we could
be her renters.

"That will be fine," she said.

Kathy murmured in her ear, "Shouldn't they have a lease?"

Michi replied in full voice, "They don't need a lease. I trust
them more than I trust myself."

Wowee! The deal was sealed. We rented apartment 403 as
snowbirds for twenty years. Her son, Randy, lives in Honolulu and
managed the apartment, always making wonderful upgrades. He's
a professional cabinetmaker and became our friend and general
contractor for renovations when we bought our own apartment in
the same building .

Sadly, we never got to see Michi again. She returned to
California and died less than two years later in 1995. Randy gave
us a copy of the program from the memorial service. I still have it.
It's purple, her favorite color. During her terminal illness she speci-
fied that anyone attending her funeral had to wear purple. The
family gave us a memento of hers, a charming little dish with a
yellow china lily.

We also received a copy of the family's biography of Michi.
Larry and I learned about her life.

"Creak. Groan. Rattle. The walls and ceiling of that tiny
house were emitting audible protests as they began to shudder and
shake. The little Nikkei girl and her two sisters, arranged like paja-

ma-ed sardines in one of the tiny beds, showed initial alarm, then settled back down to sleep. It was just Papa again driving his truck with the house hitched up behind him, moving his family and their meager belongings in the middle of the night. Being the children of a poor Japanese truck farmer, by now they had gotten used to going to sleep in one locale and waking up the next morning in a totally different nearby city. This was a habitual hardship, and not simply a result of her family's poverty. Always having to move to more fertile land made it difficult for Michi to establish friendships. She was always changing schools and neighborhoods....but that little girl learned that there are always ways to cope so long as you don't stop trying....

"As a truck farmer Papa would rent several acres from a farmer and raise enough vegetables, celery, and sugar beets to cover his costs and feed his eight children. Together with their parents, they labored in the fields during the day and at night managed to squeeze into the confines of that 'mobile' home Papa had built himself. Michi would never forget having dirt for a floor...."

Her enterprising father switched to raising flowers and by the late Thirties became known as the Sweetpea King, a respected member of the Southern California Florists Association.

Michi had never had a date, but was introduced to a young nurseryman who owned a successful business. They married in 1940 and settled down in San Leandro, California. Bob designed and built a beautiful home for Michi. "She was overwhelmed by the luxury of hardwood floors underfoot. Not dirt. This house wasn't going anywhere in the middle of the night."

But history took an ugly turn. Only three months later, the Japanese bombed Pearl Harbor. The young couple, along with 120,000 other Japanese Americans living on the West Coast, were evacuated to concentration camps. "Virtually overnight, the comfort and security of her new home were replaced by the uncivilized confines of the horse stables at Tanforan Race Track in San Bruno." Michi was nine months pregnant! Two days after being herded into the stables, she gave birth to their first child, Judie Naruo....Judie was the first child born in the internment camps.

Three months later, they were all transferred to a permanent place of incarceration in Topaz, Utah. Michi, Bob, and baby Judie were assigned a tarpaper-walled barracks, with about ten families having to share one large room. Life was harsh. Temperatures ranged from 106 degrees in the summer to -30 degrees in the winter. Somehow they survived there for three years. In 1945 when Japan surrendered, they were released and made their way back to San Leandro. Expecting the worst as they approached what had been their beautiful home, they discovered their friends had taken care of it for them."

(Larry and I did get to meet Judie one winter, when she was visiting from California. A lovely lady, it was she to whom we sent our rent checks. I always included a personal note with our check. I discovered years later that she kept them all.)

Michi devoted herself to their four children, but also became a successful businesswoman. She inherited her father's gift for growing flowers, and especially loved orchids. She began her own business, Flowers by Michi. Her creations were in high demand in two shops for thirteen years. "She had pursued her passion. She had found her niche."

Michi Naruo "never lost her ability to dream about a better tomorrow."

Windows on Our World

In the early 1960s in New York, my first husband and I rented a little apartment on elegant, tree-lined East Sixty-Second Street. It was a huge upgrade from our third-floor walkup in a dilapidated building. The final straw that compelled us to move was a boisterous Friday night party in the flat above us. Around midnight, we heard the ear-splitting sound of breaking glass. A party guest had dived through the window and fallen four stories. We looked out our window and saw the young man, perhaps about twenty, lying on his back on the sidewalk, dying. A drug overdose? Suicide? We never found out.

Our new uptown rent was the massive sum of $160 a month. The problem was, with our low-paying jobs, we couldn't afford it! I had many anxiety-filled moments, like announcing to my husband, "Getting your pants pressed cost a dollar!"

Across the street was a freshly painted white townhouse. Somehow we discovered that it was owned by world-famous Bennett Cerf, cofounder and publisher of Random House, also a celebrity panelist on the game show *What's My Line?* One Saturday night it appeared that Mr. Cerf was having a party. We just happened to look out our living room window at 2:00 a.m. to see three guests leaving Mr. Cerf's townhouse: author Truman Capote with a beautiful girl on each arm.

That was the closest we got to the New York literary world.

Chapter 7
ON BEING A GRANDMA

"I love being a grandma. It's like eating all the ice cream you want and never getting fat."

—**Cissy Spacek** as Sally Rayburn in *Bloodlines*

Our Marvelous Family
(Yes, I'm Gushing)

First I want to tell you about my two stepdaughters, who are like my own daughters now. I still, after thirty-three years, wrestle with the terminology. Should I call them "my daughters" or "my stepdaughters"? At this very moment, the outrageous idea that I need to make such a decision brings me to tears. In my chapter on MIRIAM, I will tell you all about Miriam Luby Wolfe, my only child, and how I lost her.

Larry and I were married thirteen months after we met. Second marriages are known to create emotional challenges. Siblings can be jealous of the new wife. They often feel threatened. Will they lose their inheritance? Or the attention and love their father has always bestowed on them?

I lucked out, big time. Larry's daughters, Jackie Lau and Myrna Spurrier, were both married and had fulfilling lives of their own. Both are exceptional women: kind, generous, and loving. We have one tragic fact in common: both my mother and theirs died of cancer at the age of forty-eight.

Jackie and Myrna welcomed me. I never knew their mother, Hannah, but obviously she was an extraordinary woman. From her hospital bed, she told the girls that Larry would need a new companion; that he shouldn't live his life alone. "And when he finds someone, be nice!"

Over the years I have been constantly reminded of what remarkable parents Larry and Hannah were. I see it in Jackie and Myrna, who is two-and-a-half years younger. They are both gifted professional artists and art teachers, yet they are not competitive. Quite the opposite. They have always been supportive of each other. Lending each other tools for art projects. Exchanging ideas. Myrna taking Jackie's UH Outreach class in Bronze Casting and even assisting some of the other students.

They have transmitted the same quality of generosity and unconditional love to their children.

73

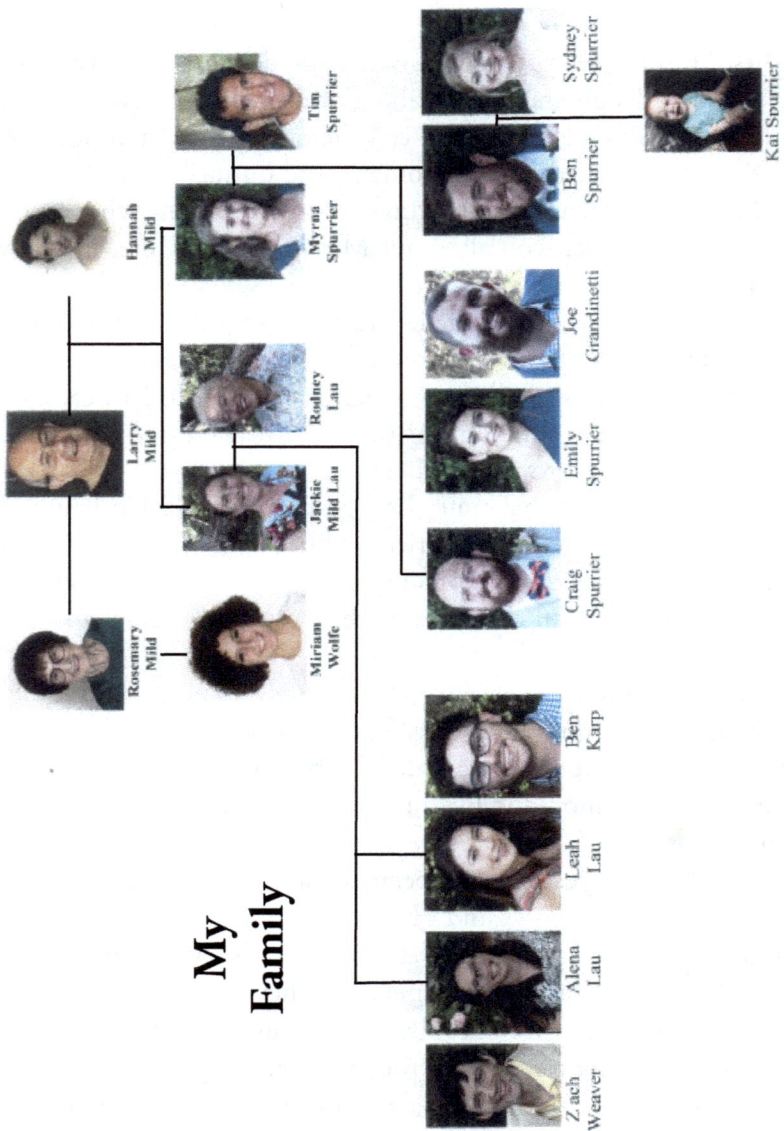

My Family

We have five marvelous grandchildren (See "My Family" on page 74):

Alena Grace Lau and Leah Michelle Lau are the daughters of Jackie and Rodney Lau. Craig Timothy Spurrier; Benjamin Lawrence Spurrier; and Emily Hannah Spurrier are the children of Myrna and Tim Spurrier.

Our great-grandson, Kai Benjamin Spurrier, the world's happiest baby, was born December 2, 2019, son of Ben and Sydney. "Kai" means "sea" in Hawaiian.

I promise not to write 200 pages about how astonishing, brilliant, talented, and loving they all are. (Only a hundred pages—just kidding.)

For both the Laus and Spurriers, life is a family affair. While the girls were growing up, Larry taught them skills in carpentry, as well as handling plumbing and electrical problems. They both learned quickly. Now Jackie helps Rodney renovate his rental houses. When Tim, as head of a private school here, launched an annual Pumpkin Festival, the whole Spurrier family pitched in, including the making and selling of 800 servings of lemonade.

A Grandma's Dilemma

We were sitting at the kitchen table in our house in Severna Park, Maryland, in 1993. The Laus were visiting from Honolulu.

"I wish you were my mother," said our five-year-old granddaughter Alena.

"You'd be happy about that for about five minutes," I answered.

I had mixed feelings about her telling me. I was pleased that she enjoyed being around me so much, but I didn't want it to be at her mother's expense.

"I like being at your house," she said.

"Why?" I asked.

"'Cuz you don't tell me what to do all the time like Nanny does." (The girls' great-grandmother lived with them.)

Alena was already a talented artist. I could tell. She was drawing in the thick spiral notebook her mother had given her.

"I wish I could draw these animals better."

"Mom'll show you how," I said.

"She doesn't teach me things. She teaches the other kids at the Academy."

How do I explain? Alena isn't in Jackie's formal art classes at the Art Center of the Honolulu Academy of Arts; she's in a class there with a different teacher. But as her mother, Jackie teaches her every day of the week. Every time she shows Alena how to do something, she's teaching her. But I didn't tell Alena that. I thought it would sound too preachy, and if I preached I would create a gulf between us.

Besides, mothers are always the last ones to get credit from their kids—if they ever get credit. Why is that? Is it that familiarity breeds disrespect? Or do they admire their mothers secretly but don't want to show it because, if they do show it, they'll feel too dependent?

Mea Kelpie
The Hazards of Bragging Rights

In June of 2004 two stone lions welcomed Larry and me as we mounted the steps to the Corcoran Gallery of Art in Washington, D.C. We'd come for the opening of the National Scholastic Arts and Writers Exhibition, sponsored by the Alliance for Young Artists & Writers, Inc. Each state runs its own annual regional competition. The 1,200 honorees at the Corcoran were chosen from the 250,000 regional winners. We had a personal stake in this show. One of the winners was a sculpture titled *The Kelpie,* created by

Alena, a sophomore at Roosevelt High School in Honolulu.

After wine and hors d'oeuvres, we entered the first exhibit room, and there against the back wall stood a chest-high glass case containing small ceramics. *The Kelpie* was on the far right and depicted a young girl crouching beside a rippling pond, with a horse up to its neck in the blue-green water.

"This is our granddaughter's piece," I announced proudly to the parade of visitors. They all stopped to look. And then I grandly interpreted it, paraphrasing the definition from *Merriam-Webster's Collegiate Dictionary*. "The kelpie—the little girl—is a water sprite of Scottish folklore who delights in the drowning of wayfarers." Visitors seemed to appreciate my explanation, because none of the artworks bore one. Many visitors took pictures. Speaking of pictures, I had called the Corcoran in advance to ask whether they allowed cameras. "No, only in the reception area." Being obsessively obedient since I was a little girl, I didn't bring mine. We got there and almost every visitor had one! A kindly looking woman approached and I whipped up my courage:

"If you'd be willing to take a couple pictures of our granddaughter's sculpture and send them to us, we'll send you an autographed copy of our mystery novel."

"I love mysteries," she said, "but I'll go you one better. My sister is here with an extra throw-away camera and we'll give it to you." She even refused to let us pay for it. What a lovely lady. (We sent her a book, of course.) So I took umpteen pictures, not just of Alena's sculpture, but in all three rooms as a record of the fine quality of the entire exhibit (as well as excerpts of writings on easels).

I held court at the Corcoran for two hours. And for the entire year after, I carried pictures in my purse, doing show-and-tell to all family, friends, and even the remotest acquaintances. Nobody escaped.

Until Alena's mom heard me. We were all attending a large holiday party, when Jackie said in a stern voice that every guest could hear: "No, Rosemary, you've got it wrong! The *horse* is the kelpie!"

Huh? What? Oh, no! Here's what happened. I had indeed

looked up "kelpie" in the dictionary, but I neglected to also read the origin of the word in brackets: from the Scottish-Gaelic "heifer or colt." (You've heard the Latin phrase *mea culpa*, meaning "my fault." Well, *mea* kelpie!)

Since then I've promised Alena I'll always write down her own interpretations of her artworks. No improvising. Fortunately, my humiliating goof had no lasting impact. The sponsors of the competition bought *The Kelpie* for their offices in New York.

Don't Try To Stop Me

Now, please don't try to stop me from telling you the details about our five grandchildren and first great-grandchild. It won't work! So here goes.

Leah

Memorable quotes:

In her early teens:

"Trying to explain anything to eighth graders is like trying to explain photosynthesis to a walnut."

When she opened our birthday present, an electric nail buffer, she said: "Somebody got into my head. It's just what I wanted."

"I think if you have a Jewish nose you should love and cherish it."

At Roosevelt High, Leah was already focused on her future profession. While on the track team she helped the trainers. (Jackie and I held our breath watching her win the 300-meter hurdles.) At the University of San Francisco she majored in Exercise and Sport Science, specializing in kinesiology.

During her four college years, she had a part-time job babysitting twin boys from the age of six weeks. Here's a "small-world" coincidence. The twins' mother used to live in Severna Park and knew my daughter at Severna Park High School. She was a class ahead of Miriam.

Leah is now a Doctor of Physical Therapy. She also has post-doctoral credentials as a Certified Functional Manual Therapist. In 2020 Leah and her fiancé, Ben Karp, moved to Honolulu, where she continues practicing Physical Therapy. Ben has launched a real estate career. Sadly, because of COVID-19, we hardly ever get to see them. Leah has many PT patients, and she worries that these contacts could cause health problems for Larry and me because of our ages and our own medical issues.

She and Ben live with Jackie and Rodney. In July, all nine of us family members celebrated my birthday at the Laus, where, mindful of COVID-19, they set up three tables and observed social distancing. But now, as the pandemic refuses to end, we are all more cautious. Only two come to our apartment at a time; all four of us wear masks when not eating and observe social distancing.

Two family members at the Laus' are oblivious to social distancing—Ben and Leah's dogs: Moose, a chocolate lab; and Marley, a sprawling, affectionate (and rambunctious) mix. They have the run (or squeeze) of the comfortably crowded house.

Leah is highly organized. She calls herself a "minimalist" and, early on at her parents' house, loved to throw out anything she thought was extraneous to make room for her and Ben's stuff. (Never mind that it belonged to her mother.) Jackie and Rodney are just the opposite: collectors/accumulators. Jackie has some logic to her side of it. As an artist, she knows that sooner or later that "thing," whatever the object is, might find a use, either incorporated into one of her artworks or as a gizmo for creating one. At first there was no meeting of minds between mother and daughter. A truce developed when Leah promised to ask Jackie first for permission to throw something out.

Alena

Memorable quotes:

In the fall of 1994 Jackie accepted a fabulous commission for the Bishop Museum's exhibition honoring the *Hawaii Loa* sailing ship: celebrating the heritage and triumphs of Native Hawaiian voyagers. The exhibition was to run from January to June 1995. Her assignment was four life-size figures: the sail maker, the navigator and two canoe builders. She was creating all the sculptures in her home studio, just a few steps downstairs. Naturally, the work required hundreds of hours over a period of about two months. As Larry and I were carpooling Alena and her friends home from preschool, we heard her talking in the back seat. "My mother has been gone for a year."

Alena in high school:

"TV has turned my mind into a mental landfill."

When I splashed stew off the counter in our Honolulu kitchen, she said, "Grandma, you're sharing gravy with the floor."

About her conversations with a friend: "When she speaks, it's a thesis with supporting details, and she ends with 'In conclusion.'"

Alena chose, like her sister, to become a Doctor of Physical Therapy. Alena and Zach Weaver, her fiancé, own a home in Bremerton, Washington, a half-hour ferry ride from Seattle. From the ferry, Zach rides his bike to his highly skilled job at a glass factory. Alena works at Kitsap Physical Therapy, specializing in the treatment of neurological disorders. (A bit of trivia: Kitsap County, Washington, was named for Chief Kitsap of the Suquamish tribe.)

Craig

Memorable quotes:

I was reading a book to Craig titled *Inside the Human Body*—one of the books in *The Magic Schoolbus* series He was six and wanted to know where the kidneys were. Before I could answer, he'd found the picture himself.

"Don't you know *anything?*" he asked me.

I sighed and said nothing. I know that schools and parents try hard to instill self-esteem in children. Well, by the time Craig was done with me, I was the one needing the self-esteem lessons.

Tim and Myrna started a private school in the town of Waimea on the Big Island of Hawaii. Some of their students were children of scientists at the famed Keck Observatory atop Mauna Kea. At a faculty-parent cookout, Craig began a debate with a guest. Before long, our nine-year-old grandson was looking up at a tall Keck astronomer and telling him, "I can prove you wrong."

Years later, when the family eventually moved to Honolulu. Craig worked as an IT Specialist at the University of Hawaii-Manoa. But I report with tearful mixed emotions that he has just started a new Mainland job: in Richmond at Virginia Commonwealth University, where he is the Assistant Director of Research Information Systems.

Here in Honolulu Craig also had an avocation—as a caterer. He and Joe Grandinetti (our granddaughter Emily's long-term boyfriend and former chef) cooked our Temple Emanu-El dinner for 250 on the second night of Passover two years ago. The whole Spurrer family helped. Myrna and Emily made up the plates; Tim did dishes.

Craig and Joe (who is like a family member now) recently catered a small "Gender Reveal Party." Larry and I seem to have been born on an outdated planet. We didn't know this is a millennials' event for finding out the sex of a friend's baby still in the womb. Tucked inside the cupcakes was surprise pink frosting.

Ben

Ben began young riding quarter horses. He competed in cutting and reining; at age seventeen, at one point ranking eighth in the world in his age group.

When he and Sydney married in 2017, he began his true calling: as a craftsman in Charleston, South Carolina. In his business, called Burls and Steel, he creates hand-forged knives and wood crafts—one-of-a-kind works of art for restaurant chefs, home cooks, and hunters. Sydney handles marketing and photography. You can visit their website at **www.burlsandsteel.com.**

In December, 2020 Ben received a MADE IN THE SOUTH contest award. He won for **Outdoors Runner-Up: Burls and Steel Knives.** The awards were featured in *Garden & Guns* magazine *(Dec. 2020/Jan. 2021 issue).* The write-up says: *Even his dog knew Ben Spurrier was destined to make knives. His rescue pooch often brought the former horse trainer gorgeous deer antlers from the woods near the family farm. "They made the best knife handles," Spurrier says. He began forging blades for farm work, and soon enough he and his wife, Sydney, started selling them at farmers' markets and online.... Their Camp to Kitchen knives...move with ease from the duck camp to the countertop. Any frills the blades have come from an elevated approach to materials and design. One of the knives, for instance, features sixty-layer Damascus steel forged into a five-and-a-half-inch blade. The handle nods to Spurrier's home state—Hawaiian koa with a brass spacer, mosaic pins, and a dyed black ash bolster.* | *$300–$850.*

Emily

Emily, a talented artist, attends community college classes with the goal of entering the nursing profession. Myrna taught her to sew and Emily immediately created her own specialty: bandannas with Hawaiian patterns for doggies. She also launched her own website, **www.pineapplepups.com,** and (before COVID) sold the bandannas at a local weekend market. Emily is an avid gardener of a whole range of plants from tomatoes to cacti, and also is a proficient baker. For my last birthday dinner she made sinfully delicious chocolate pops with sprinkles. Allowing for COVID restrictions, she and Joe love the gym and hiking. Emily also competes in jiujitsu. Our conversations with them always include the latest on Odin, their gangly rescue dog who sleeps with them.

Kai

Kai is our first great-grandchild. A precious happy baby, at one year old, he has red hair, smiles all the time, and is now walking and beginning to say lots of words. Because of COVID-19 it may be a long long time before we get to see Ben, Sydney, and Kai in person. Thank heaven for FaceTime!

Raku

Raku is a traditional ceramic art form invented by the Japanese in the sixteenth century. It involves rapid firing in an open outdoor pit. The glazed hot ceramic pieces are removed with tongs and placed in an airtight container with combustible materials, producing exquisite, quite unpredictable, effects and colors. Hawaii Craftsmen holds an annual three-day camp-out for artists and their families. Artists of all ages bring their artworks for firing.

For years Jackie and Myrna successfully entered their

pieces in the juried show. When we were still snowbirds, Larry and I had three-way phone conversations between Honolulu and Severna Park. Jackie told us the *raku* ceramics were being exhibited in "Mark's garage." I thought that was just a friend's garage with a bunch of shelves. Eventually, I learned it was The ARTS at Marks Garage, a Chinatown gallery.

In 2019 *raku* was truly a family affair. The juried exhibition was held at the Windward Mall in Kailua and included beautiful pieces, not only by Jackie and Myrna, but also by Emily and Joe.

When Alena and Leah were ages eight and ten, their pieces were accepted and they were told to set their own prices. Leah priced her pot at $28.95.

Turmoil and a Legacy

Which reminds me how much in turmoil life can be. We moved to Honolulu seven years ago, and reveled in the closeness of seven family members here. Most Sunday nights we had dinner together, usually at a restaurant; sometimes in our apartment; the kids would bring in Chinese food, deli, or pizza. We got spoiled. The configuration changed a few months ago, when Myrna and Tim moved to South Carolina for Tim's new job as head of a private school. A bonus for them, because Ben, Sydney, and Kai are only fifteen minutes away. Their move has left us bereft, but, again. thank heaven for FaceTime and delightful landline chats.

We're a two-Honda family: two 2006 Honda CR-Vs. The CR-V is a small, well-designed SUV, perfect for us to haul our books to signings. We bought my red one new when we lived in Severna Park, and I drove it for seven years. The beige one we bought used in Honolulu. So when we moved here we brought mine and gave it to Myrna. She drove it for seven years, until they moved, then she gave it to Emily. So my red car is now in its third generation of family owners.

Chapter 8
HAPPY HODGEPODGE

"What are you going to do? Everything, is my guess. It will be a little messy, but embrace the mess. It will be complicated, but rejoice in the complications."—**Nora Ephron**

DISPATCH FROM A PARKING LOT ENCOUNTER
'Character Floss'—the idea has potential but still needs perfecting

Our dentist always said, "You don't have to floss all your teeth…only the ones you want to keep." Perhaps the same should be said about character flossing? [The three-line title and this italicized introduction were added to my title "Character Floss" by the *Washington Post* as my essay appeared in the Metro section, December 7, 2009.]

I was washing my hands in the ladies' room of the Bob Evans Restaurant in Breezewood, Pennsylvania. On my left, perpendicular to the sink, but a foot or two behind me, was a counter, where I had placed my *Washington Post*. No more than thirty seconds later (I swear!) I turned to pick up my paper. It was gone.

I gasped. My day was ruined.

Larry and I were on our annual summer pilgrimage from Severna Park to Akron, Ohio, to visit our clan. Breezewood was our traditional stop for breakfast and gas before heading west on the Pennsylvania Turnpike. We'd left the house at eight and, as always, I grabbed the *Post* out of our box at the curb and threw it in the car. I had scanned the front section over Bob Evans' fluffy pancakes.

I dashed out of the ladies' room, jerking to a stop at the gift shop counter. "Somebody took my *Washington Post!*" I blurted out to the gray-haired clerk. "Did you happen to see a woman carrying a newspaper?" Her Bob Evans-trained smile remained fixed, but her vocal chords refused to respond. Maybe she was contemplating calling Security—not to catch a thief, but to remove this crazy customer from the premises.

I didn't wait to find out. Threading my way among the sparkly pastel shirts and buckwheat neck pillows, I plunged out the door. In the parking lot just a few feet ahead, I spotted a woman in a pink pants outfit about to climb into her car.

"Excuse me," I trilled. "Did you happen to see a *Washington Post* in the ladies' room?"

The lady turned to face me. She looked to be about fifty, several inches shorter than I, and had a sweet, round face and rimless glasses. "Oh, no!" she wailed. "I just assumed someone left it there on purpose and I thought, Well, I'd love to read the *Washington Post*. I'm soooo sorry." She ducked the top half of herself into the back seat and retrieved my paper.

"Thank you so much," I gushed. "That's very kind of you." I tucked the paper under my arm and sprinted to our minivan, where Larry sat with the motor running. He gave me a funny look. "What was that all about?"

"You don't want to know," I muttered.

And that's the whole point. What had come over me, anyway? At what instant had I turned into a possessive banshee? What was I thinking, humiliating that poor defenseless lady? The daily *Post* costs thirty-five cents (even less when you're a subscriber, as we have been for twenty years). I could have accessed it online at our sister-in-law's in Akron. But that would not have been the same as having the tangible pages spread out before me. After all, the *Washington Post* is our daily breakfast guest, and I had barely begun to read it.

But none of this matters. What does matter is that this incident exposed me: *I have a character flaw*. And that's where my proposed invention enters the picture.

I plan to invent "character floss"—to get rid of character flaws. It will be a packet of theoretical (or slightly magical) string or some other device that can perform on the same principle as dental floss. I'll use it to flick out my obnoxious behaviors the same way I floss my teeth after breakfast. With character floss I can hone my personality to be so benevolent that, in the future, I will let the dear lady in the parking lot keep my *Post*. In fact, I won't even consider hunting her down.

This invention has such great potential that I'll market it

to the whole world and donate the proceeds to hungry children everywhere. However, I do foresee one problem.

What if the device can be used to floss out not just your own character flaws, but someone else's? What if a friend or family member chooses to eliminate my talkativeness—a behavior that I'm fond of, that I've lived with my whole life and cherish?

As you can see, my invention needs perfecting. But please be patient. I'm working on it.

A Free T-Shirt Has Its Price

I wrote this piece way back in 1997 and published it in The Publick Enterprise, *July 1997. Larry and I were living in Severna Park, forty-five minutes from Bowie, Maryland, where the Baltimore Orioles AA Farm team played. It was a delight to attend the Bowie Baysox games with friends, spur of the moment, a casual neighborhood spectacle. I even got to know some of the players' wives and published an article about them in* Washington Woman. *How the wives, many from the Dominican Republic, became fast friends for months and then abruptly left when a few of the husbands got lucky, chosen for "The Show," the Major League Orioles. Now in 2021 the Double-A Baysox are still there!*

I'm waiting patiently in line at the Bowie Baysox box office. The prospect of seats right behind the on-deck circle makes my heart leap higher than a pop fly. I'm a hot dog and hollerin' Baysox fan, overjoyed that our nearby Baltimore Orioles AA farm team is holding its own in its Eastern League division.

But a bigger challenge than the allure of the team's won-lost column awaits me personally. This summer, will I have the fortitude to resist the ballpark freebie offers—the seductive treats that tempt me?

You see, I'm no stranger to such temptations. One balmy

night last July, Larry and I headed into Prince George's Stadium for a Baysox game. On the way to our seats, I spotted long tables covered with clipboards. Hawkers were calling out "A free Baysox T-shirt! Just sign up for a credit card." My husband kept walking. I thought hard for a split second. I didn't need or want a new credit card and I'd never use this one. But a Baysox T-shirt would be worth it. Wouldn't it?

"Yes!" I dove for the tables and the application blanks, scribbled the minimum and received my T-shirt—snappy white with orange and green lettering. The Baysox lost, but I was happy with my new souvenir.

One week later I received a letter from the sponsoring bank. They had opened my credit card account. I filed the letter. The card arrived. But two weeks afterward, I received another letter from the bank. They had opened a second account for me. A second card arrived. A knot began growing in the pit of my stomach. Soon I received a third letter. "We apologize for mistakenly opening two accounts in your name. We have closed one. Throw the first card away."

But now I'd had enough. These people didn't know their digits from their magnetic strips. I called the Customer Service number and pleasantly said: "Please close my account."

I expected the response to be "Certainly, ma'am." But no, this was a personal approach bank. "What can we do to make things right?" the lady asked, her voice quavering.

"Nothing. Just close my account."

"Let me transfer you to my supervisor."

"No thank you." But it was too late. He came on.

"Please close my account," I said.

He gasped. "Are you sure? Isn't there anything we can do to change your mind?"

"No"

He began to cry. "Perhaps we could arrange a personal meeting. We'll do lunch."

"Oh, no," I wailed. "Are you going to ask for visitation

rights to my card?"

"That would be nice," he sobbed.

"Thank you," I said, "but this divorce is final."

"Well, okay. But if you change your mind, I'll be here."

That was the end of it—or so I thought. But a month later, I received another letter that a third account had been opened in my name. I popped four Maalox tablets and threw the letter away. Another week passed and this time I received a sackcloth-and-ashes letter from the vice president of the Credit Card Division.

"You must think we're terrible people and don't know how to run a bank. The letter you just received saying we opened a third account in your name isn't true. We didn't. Can you ever forgive us? Your single account is still in place."

I sighed. My account is flourishing. To close it will probably take an act of Congress.

So I'm standing in line at the box office with a certain apprehension. Will this season offer similar freebies? Will it be the same bank? I'm determined to cover my bases; I'll think twice about applying for a credit card I don't need just to get a free Baysox T-shirt.

On the other hand, if it's a really *nice* shirt…

P.S. I have a whole dresser full of free T-shirts.

Whispers from Corporate Cubicles
My Filching Project

I had a fabulous job in New York at a prestigious magazine. I edited the Letters to the Editor, read unsolicited manuscripts, and edited articles accepted for publication. It was an honor to work there. My colleagues, from editor-in-chief down, were a brilliant, scholarly group who considered editing and rewriting a fine art, like polishing a marble sculpture.

One spring day in 1965, I got to the office so early the

lights hadn't been turned on yet. In the gray morning gloom, I heard a rustle as I neared my desk. Emerging from the book review editor's office was a senior editor, carrying several books.

"Morning!" I chirped.

"Good morning. You're in early I see."

"Yes, I have a pile of work and decided to get a head start."

She nodded and that was the end of the conversation.

But during the next few hours, I pieced together the scenario, the behind-the-scenes reality. The senior editor was carrying review copies of new books. Wowee! You see, the book review editor had an enormous desk, maybe six feet square. At least a hundred books sat on that desk. Each month all the major publishers sent her advance copies of their forthcoming books. A review in our magazine was BIG, even if only a few paragraphs. The number of review copies received was kind of laughable because we only published a few small reviews each month. So what did management do with the rest of the copies? Rumor had it they were sold to a used bookstore. Which the publishers did not sanction. Perhaps it was just a rumor. But it made sense nonetheless.

I sat down at my desk and drifted into a marvelous thought process. If that senior editor was helping herself to a few books, maybe everyone on the staff was. And why shouldn't they? So why shouldn't I? And there began my own Filching Project. But not just anything. No novel or self-help book that I could afford to pick up at any bookstore. Oh, no. I chose only exotic art books. So what's on my shelf today in Honolulu fifty-five years later? Beautiful volumes: *Impressionism, Redon, World Furniture, The Tate Gallery, Modern Painting,* and *The Flowering of the Renaissance.*

A few weeks later, my now ex-husband and I moved to Maryland for his new job with the Federal Government. That ended my New York career and my short-lived, successful venture in larceny.

More Whispers from the Corporate World

After our move to Maryland, I worked for a Baltimore publisher of medical and scientific books and journals—as a copy editor and eventually as managing editor of a chemical association journal. Our metal partitions were supposed to give us privacy. My next-door coworker seemed to think she was on a desert island. At 9:30 one Monday morning, she was on the phone to her doctor's office.

"I need to speak to the doctor immediately. My fourteen-year-old daughter was at a weekend party at a hotel and she got gang-banged. Should she be getting an AIDS test?"

This was in 1986 during the AIDS epidemic. Apparently, my coworker thought none of us were listening, but how could we help it? Voices floated above and around the partitions. I never got to find out the doctor's answer. Darn it!

For six months or so, our department was installed in an ancient building, in one vast echoing room with a sinking floor and only single-stall ladies' and men's bathrooms—for fifty of us. After three months, one of the vice presidents burst in and virtually stamped his foot in our supervisor's office. "I am noting an excessive use of toilet paper in the women's bathroom. They must be taking rolls home!" Can you believe it?

I worked with an artist who was designing a magazine cover for me. She was a petite, white-faced woman with rimless glasses and brown hair severely pulled back in a ponytail. She was an excellent artist, but always appeared to be frightened. Her body almost recoiled when I spoke to her. I asked myself: Am I being too aggressive, too demanding? Anyway, one day we got to talking.

"What does your husband do?" I asked her.

"Prison guard," she whispered.

This job—for the medical and scientific publisher—was actually the perfect job for me and I'm deeply grateful to the company. I worked as a "home worker," which was wonderful because my daughter, Miriam, was two years old and too young for day care. I kept track of my hours (and was mindful of deadlines). Once a week I delivered an envelope of my completed work to another employee, who also happened to live in Severna Park. I would leave my envelope inside her screen door, and there was always a fresh envelope for me for my next week's assignment. She had a darling dog named Missy, in the pen attached to the house. Miriam loved petting Missy. It was the highlight of her day. After thirteen years I became a full-time employee, still copyediting for such publications as *Pediatrics* and *The Journal of Occupational Medicine*, and at the same time I was managing editor of *Chemical Times & Trends*.

I applied for a new job. A letter arrived. "Come for an interview." I tingled with excitement. A huge, multinational corporation.

I read on. Before going for my interview I was to report to the nurse in another building for "a drug test." A drug test? Oh my God. What had I done to deserve this? Taking Advil for Colds and Sinuses for three days was my limit. I donned my navy blue good-luck suit with gray and blue patterned blouse, and grabbed my briefcase containing my resume and copies of the medical and scientific journals I had edited. After parking, I waited for the corporate shuttle bus for transport to The Nurse.

Friendly she wasn't. All in white, with nurse's cap, a severe expression, already-accusing eyes, and anger lines emanating from the corners of her mouth. Visions of Nurse Ratched in *One Flew Over the Cuckoo's Nest* flashed through my mind. Nurse Gestapo said, "Follow me" and led me to the bathroom. I was to pee into the special cup she handed me. Groan. *In my good suit I have to do this? Okay. It will soon be over.*

But it wasn't. I assumed I'd be in the bathroom alone. Oh,

no. Nurse Gestapo came in with me and stood by the door, beefy arms crossed over her chest. The toilet was only a few feet away. I couldn't pee. After five minutes I managed to produce a few dribbles and held up the sterile cup. "This okay?" I asked.

"No! That's not nearly enough," she snapped.

Her antagonizing demeanor killed the deal. I could not produce even one more drop. She looked at her watch in annoyance and said, "Go to your interview. Come back afterward." In abject embarrassment, I slunk out. As the friendly secretary ushered me to the shuttle, I blurted out my failure. "I couldn't pee!" She smiled. "Don't worry, you're not the only one. See you later."

I went to my interview feeling degraded and sloppy, like I needed another shower. Despite my misery, I got the job. Back on the shuttle bus, I entered the nurse's sanctum. The secretary greeted me and pointed to a corner table laden with pots of coffee, sodas, and donuts. "Help yourself," she said. For an hour I gulped caffeine, alternating between Diet Coke and coffee. With my belly expanding and distended, I heard Nurse Gestapo calling my name. This time, despite her forbidding presence, my body cooperated. I managed to pee the required amount.

I started work two weeks later. During one lunch hour, I confided my drug test ordeal to a colleague. She listened with rapt attention. But I noticed it was not with recognition and understanding as if she too had been through it. That's when I discovered that the drug test for a prospective hire was a new corporate policy. In this office of fourteen, I was the only one required to take it.

Ta da! In the little conference room where our immediate boss held our weekly meetings, he announced, "Corporate has initiated an **Economy Drive**. From now on, if you want a new pencil you first have to turn in your old stub." He couldn't continue. We were nearly rolling on the floor, doubled up laughing.

Then Corporate launched the **Ethics Drive**. Another edict. No outside contractor was allowed to bring us treats. One of our top-quality vendors produced slides, viewgraphs, and other presentation tools for us. On Saint Patrick's Day every year he brought us green bagels in appreciation of our business. Big expense, fourteen green bagels. And cream cheese! Oh my God. The edict was in place. No more bagels for us.

During that Ethics Drive, one of the senior executives was giving special assignments to the Typing and Graphics departments. But not for the company. For his wife, who was working on her master's degree.

Then we had the **Economy Drive** commingled with the **Ethics Drive**. In previous years we had always been ushered into the conference room during work time for a twenty-minute ethics video. But now we were no longer allowed to spend the twenty minutes of work time watching it. So how did Corporate decide to inform us of the Ethics update? By manufacturing thousands of videotapes, acted out by employees, and mailing them for us to view at home. That was their idea of saving money.

Mine arrived in our curbside mailbox. In a spirit of uncharacteristic rebellion, I walked it straight to the backyard and threw it in the garbage can. The next day, our supervisor asked me if I'd watched it.

Without waiting for an answer, he asked, "How did you like my acting?"

Oops. "You were good, Ted, just fine."

Still, I loved the job, the fast-paced challenges, the rewards—for instance, when I prepared a presentation for an engineer to give in South Korea, and he called me from Seoul to tell me it went well.

Larry and I were both in defense industries, although different companies. Even as newlyweds, we understand each other's long hours and work stresses. So in 1993 he surprised me by choosing to retire early from his forty-plus years as a design engineer—

to spend the winters in Honolulu. Feeling quite upbeat and important, I went to our Human Resources Department and asked the director, "What is it called when you retire after six-and-a-half years?"

A flicker of amusement crossed his face as he said: "It's called quitting."

Is It Yours?

For sixteen years Larry and I held a picnic on Monday of Memorial Day weekend at our home in Severna Park. It started out the first year with twenty-five friends and family and ended with seventy-five. The long hours—from 11:00 a.m. to 10:00 p.m.—worked well; we were never overcrowded. Guests dropped in at all hours and stayed as long as they wanted. Even at ten o'clock, as the last guests were drifting to their cars, one friend's nine-year-old daughter came running back into the house, refusing to go home, because she was having so much fun.

The dining room table was always laden with goodies. Our specialty was Empire Kosher Barbecued Turkey. Our homemade chili, accompanied by rice, was our own creation: a six-pound can of Stagg chili to which we added browned hamburger, sautéed onions, and mushrooms. We also served the most un-Kosher honey-baked ham, plus side dishes and desserts.

We had a large screened back porch and, one year, our guests got a bonus attraction. A pair of house sparrows had built a nest under an eave and given birth! All day long our guests watched Mom and Dad flying back and forth to the nest to feed their hungry newborns.

A week before one party, I felt overwhelmed by housework, so I hired a cleaning service. The two women did a superb job.

The day after the picnic I opened the front hall closet and saw something strange. A long, forest-green London Fog raincoat, probably owned by a tall woman. It was quite new-looking. London Fogs were expensive; this one may have cost at least $100. I took it off the hanger to inspect it, hoping to find some kind of ID. In one of the deep pockets I discovered a set of keys! No car key, but a whole bunch of others, maybe even house keys, and no tag of any sort with a name on it.

I called the cleaning service, assuming their records would show which workers had come to our house. They would call the women and the owner of the coat could come and retrieve it. The manager's response shocked me. "They don't work here anymore."

"But...but..." I stumbled, "they were just here a few days ago." He was evasive. I guessed the two women left the company to start their own cleaning service and he didn't want to reveal their names because I might hire them instead. (He would've been right about that.) It also occurred to me that they'd have turned in their work records and may not have had any way to retrace their steps.

So now what? I began calling all our women friends who had come to the picnic. I described the coat. "Is it yours?" "No." In my heart I knew none of them were that tall and none had arrived in a raincoat. It had been a warm and sunny day.

For three years—yes, three years—the coat sat in the front hall closet. Our friend who'd visited from New York said to me on the phone, "This is the third time you've asked me."

Finally, mystery unsolved, I donated it to Goodwill, keys and all.

Epiphany in Lordstown

Every year we visited George and Mitzie Mild in Akron, Ohio—one year with Myrna, Tim, and our three small grandchildren. My brother-in-law arranged a special treat. He took us all to the General Motors Assembly Plant in Lordstown, Ohio. We sat in the little tram cars tooling around the manufacturing business of assembling Chevrolet Cavaliers. The grandchildren were bored silly, but I could have stayed all day watching the robots perform some of the complex tasks.

As our tram passed a group of mechanics diligently at work, bent over the steel frames, they stopped—and turned to wave at us, friendly-like. But immediately I had a churlish, negative thought. *I'm not going to buy a Cavalier coming off the line today. Those guys are distracted. The car might have a bolt missing.*

One Saturday a few months later, I was browsing through our local paper and my eyes landed on an article in the weekly automotive section. The reporter wrote: "The Chevy Cavalier is the most mediocre car GM ever produced."

I read it aloud to Larry. "See?" I said. "It's because they waved to us."

Sitting in the Middle

I'm sitting on the plane between two strangers, both men. Larry and I are flying to Seattle on our way to a tour of the Canadian Rockies, and it's the first time ever that we haven't been able to sit together. Somehow our coach reservations got messed up.

Larry is in seat B on the aisle; I'm stuck in seat D in the middle across the aisle from him. Our plane hasn't left the gate yet. I'm about to read my book and suddenly I'm self-conscious about my bookmark. It's Michelangelo's *David*. Yes, I'm self-conscious about it even though David is wearing an illustrator's painted-on fig leaf. Somehow it seems prurient in my physical situation, between these two men, as if I'm on an island in the middle of the Pacific away from Larry.

I really want to ask the passenger on my left to switch places with me so Larry and I can at least talk, but I feel awkward about imposing on a total stranger, especially because he's all business, not even saying hello. He's thirtyish, in a gray suit and open-necked striped Oxford shirt. As the flight attendant gives her safety spiel, I turn my head. Larry asks me what's wrong. "Just looking for the exits," I say softly. The businessman smiles at me very slightly. I assume he understands that Larry is my husband or at least my traveling companion, but he makes no offer to switch seats.

This is totally not good. When I sit in the window seat next to Larry I can comfortably and surreptitiously do things, like quickly running a toothbrush over my teeth without paste or blowing my nose. But trapped between two strangers, these insignificant actions balloon into drama.

The suit on my left pulls out his laptop, a classy model with a large screen, and sets it on his tray table. His right elbow hits my left arm. I pull it away, trying not to do it nastily. Now I can't use my armrest. Does he notice? If he does, does he even care? My right-hand seatmate looks young, twenty maybe, with a black goatee, which looks ridiculous against his fresh-skinned baby face. His Minnesota Twins baseball cap is on backwards. He's dozing off, but has left his chair in the upright position, so he keeps falling forward, seatbelt still buckled, and occasionally jerks his head up. Doesn't he know his seat can recline? Well, I'm not going to tell him!

Then there's another situation. Except during lunch, I always recline my seat. After we're sky-borne, I recline my seat as usual, when I feel a tap on my shoulder. "Excuse me." I twist my head around and see an Asian man and his companion, both in dark suits, white shirts, and ties. "Could you put your seat straight up, please? I need to use my laptop and can't when your seat is reclined."

What? "Sorry," I say. "I can't. I get backaches if I leave my seat upright during a flight." The nerve. I feel quite self-righteous, and I'm tempted to scold him as if he was ten years old. "Young man, this wouldn't be happening if you'd done your homework last night like you were supposed to." But I don't.

I want to get my notebook out of my purse, but this innocuous act presents a challenge. My purse is on the floor under the seat in front of me, next to my carry-on tote. But my tray table is open with my Diet Sprite can and plastic cup sitting on it, both full. Very slowly, I inch forward in my seat, and with both feet, coax my tote toward me. Bending slightly, the tray table cutting into my belly, I reach down, unzip the tote and un-Velcro the front flap of my purse, yanking out my notebook and pen. Victory. Now, in tiny scribbles I begin an essay, hunched over my tray table, my left arm curled around my notebook as if I'm in third grade writing a love note to Bobby Brown who sits behind me. I write extra small so the suit and baseball cap can't read it.

That's another thing. I really need to sleep, but I don't want to leave my purse on the floor in front of me. I have visions of drifting off and waking up to find my wallet and passport gone, nesting safely in the pocket of one of the men.

The only tolerable thing about my situation is that neither man wants to talk. I can't stand talking to strangers on airplanes. Once you start, you can't stop without appearing rude. You're trapped in your seat conversing when you'd rather sleep or read. Or do the *American Way* crossword puzzle. I've even had a stranger next to me give me a word. What *chutzpah*. At home in the super-market, it's okay to talk to persons you're sandwiched between at the checkout. Because you have a finite number of words you can exchange before it's your turn, there's no commitment to learn an-other shopper's history, though I do enjoy looking over their items. *Tsk tsk,* I say to myself if I see potato chips and Ho-Hos.

We get lunch. This was back in the days when the airlines actually served free food—although comedian Shelly Berman once said "airline food" is an oxymoron. On my tray is a turkey and cheese calzone, like a Hot Pocket reinforced with metal rebars. My left seatmate eats sparely, only the pocket filling and not the pack-aged cookie, which he appears to be keeping for later. I resist asking whether I can have it.

And now, how can I go to the lavatory? The tray table and laptop are open on my left, the guy's asleep on my right. Maybe I should have worn a Depend. Then Larry asks me to get out his pill. It's an anti-inflammatory, a prescription for his new knee. The flight attendant takes my lunch tray and I ask my left seatmate: "May I disturb you for a moment?" I reach over and hand Larry his pill. My seatmate says: "I would have sat over there," pointing to Larry's seat.

I realized I had to explain. "My husband had a knee replacement. He has to sit on the aisle so his right leg has extra room."

"Ouch!" says the suit, but he does not offer to trade places with me.

I keep scribbling in my notebook and finally finish my little essay: "Why I Hate Sitting in the Middle."

A Black Night To Remember
November 9, 1965, New York City, 5:15 p.m.

I entered the subway at 42nd Street and Park Avenue. With hundreds of other riders I sat down on a bench eager to get home after a long workday editing at *Harper's Magazine*, and I was beginning to chill out for the half-hour ride.

The overcrowded rush-hour subway started up, swaying this way and that, and five minutes later the conductor called out, "Houston Street." The doors opened. A few passengers exited. Ten minutes passed. We were strangers on a train, nervously silent. The car's lights were suspiciously dim. The doors were still open. Why weren't they closing? Why weren't we moving? Now the lights flickered. Now they were out! Oh, no! A solemn, authoritative conductor's voice came over the intercom.

"Ladies and Gentlemen. This subway train will not be going anywhere. We are having a power failure. The entire Northeast of the United States is blacked out. Stay calm. Leave the subway cars now. The doors are still open."

Thank heaven for that. What if our doors had already closed? They operate on power. Would we be trapped inside all night? I shuffled out onto the platform gingerly, uncertain and scared, when I heard a man's voice on my right. "Miss, I'll be glad to guide you upstairs to the street. Take my arm." I'd never seen him before and he just assumed I'd accept his offer. Of course I would.

"Thank you!" I placed my hand in the crook of his courtly right arm. What I was astonished to discover, as we slowly worked our way up each stair, was that our train was on the lowest level, in the very bowels, of the subway system. Four flights later, we emerged onto the street. I thanked this lovely gentleman profusely.

"Good luck," he said, and disappeared.

But what kind of luck? I was in *The Twilight Zone*. The sky was murky with mashed-together clouds. A sick moon tried to pierce them with weak tentacles.

A public phone booth had a line a block long with frantic callers. My husband and I had friends, an artist and his wife, in a loft on Houston Street in Greenwich Village. But which building? It was a warehouse. I couldn't remember what it looked like. All the steel doors and dingy brick facades looked alike.

Where was I? There were no street lights. No traffic lights. Cars gridlocked. Just thousands of bodies milling about. As I stood helplessly on a corner, a taxi pulled up. A passenger window rolled down.

"Where are you going?"

"Brooklyn. Cobble Hill."

"Get in. We have room."

During the two-hour ride, I opened my large paper bag of fresh rolls that I had bought at a bakery on my lunch hour, and I doled them out to the three women and the cab driver.

In *A Streetcar Named Desire*, Blanche DuBois says, "I've always depended on the kindness of strangers."

And on that black night, so did I.

I published a version of this essay in The Pen Woman, *Spring 2019, the magazine of the National League of American Pen Women, where I'm a member of the Honolulu Branch. The magazine's editor of Fiction & Nonfiction went the extra mile by including a photo inside the New York subway and the following paragraph, which she had researched.*

"Editor's note: According to an article in National Geographic, *on Nov. 9, 1965, shortly after 5 p.m. "more than 30 million people in the United States and Canada were plunged into darkness in one of the biggest electrical power failures in history." A misconfigured power line at a hydroelectric power station at Niagara Falls in Canada caused what was called 'the Great Northeast Blackout.' Neighboring power lines were quickly shut down due to overload. The blackout affected seven U.S. states as well as Ontario. More than 800,000 people who traveled on New York's subways during the peak 5 p.m. were stranded and had to walk out."*

Jazzercise

January 5th (a bunch of years ago) was a *huge* day for me at the dentist. I was finally getting my new permanent bridge of three teeth—missing from near the front of my mouth. Without them, I looked like a fugitive from a Dracula movie. With the dentist seated beside me, I was lying flat on my back, legs outstretched for the two-hour procedure. Suddenly, I felt a sharp piece of metal lodging itself on the back of my tongue—a renegade implant screw. The dentist warned, "Don't swallow!"

Instantly, I sat bolt upright. The screw flew out of my mouth. I announced, triumphantly: "It's lucky I've been doing my ab exercises!"

"Yes," he said, "you're in really good shape."

Drum roll, please! It was Jazzercise, folks! I started attending the program at home in Severna Park and continued it faithfully in Honolulu for the twenty years when we were snowbirds—and of course continue now that we live here. That day at the dentist, those ab routines we all grunt through in our floor work came to my rescue. I could've choked on that doggone screw.

* * * *

I've been going to Jazzercise for forty-one years. It satisfies my suppressed desire to be a Rockette. Jazzercise is a dance fitness franchise company founded by Judi Sheppard Missett in 1969 and headquartered in Carlsbad, California. It's forty minutes of dance, a high-intensity cardio workout, followed by twenty minutes of strength training and stretching—all set to motivating contemporary music. But in case that sounds threatening, it isn't. It's got built-in choices for us. Instructors are trained to demonstrate every dance at high impact, and then at low impact, the same intensity, but gentler. My Maryland instructor would tell us, "Don't want to jump or hop or skip? You can march. Marching is awesome!" Our fabulous instructor at the Kaimuki YMCA in Honolulu, Caroline Dang, demonstrates low impact and then says, "Do we still burn fat and calories if we do it this way? Of course we do. Listen to your body."

Jazzercise Diary: Conversations I heard before class

The class I attended in Arnold, Maryland, was held in a church sanctuary. The folding chairs for services were collapsed along the side walls. It had a cathedral ceiling, forest-green wall-to-wall carpeting, and tall stained-glass windows with gorgeous biblical scenes. The sunbeams filtering in illuminated the colors in the glass.

During my very first class, my excellent instructor, "Amanda," taught us to "spot"—the dancers' technique of fixating our eyes on one spot on the wall to give ourselves better balance. I fixed on one of the lovely stained-glass doves. Amanda gave us other important advice the first day. "Wear a sports bra so you don't break down breast tissue." Over the next few months, she also gave us delightful glimpses into her personal life. These are some of her stories.

"I'm over forty. I went to buy a Miracle Bra. But I discovered you have to have something to work with or you don't get any results. The saleslady asked me, 'Is this your first Miracle?' Well, I said, I've had two kids. How many miracles do you expect me to have in one lifetime?"

"I had an accident at home. I sat down on a chair that had had a boom box on it. The batteries had leaked out onto the chair and I didn't notice it was wet! I got first- and second-degree burns on my *tush*. I complained about the scars to my husband and he said, 'So what? Nobody'll see 'em but me and the kids.' I wasn't thrilled with his reaction."

"I was emceeing a junior high graduation. Afterward they had a 'mosh pit.' Moshing is when the kids bump into each other butt to butt. But they got more aggressive and were bouncing their heads together hard. I had to stop the music and warn them to stop moshing and stop the head butting! I could almost see those little seventh graders' brains rattling around."

"My thirteen-year-old daughter wanted an ant farm. Silly me. I ordered one and put the ants in the fridge to calm them down. When I brought them out they squirted all over the place and started biting me all over my arms. I finally collected them and this time put them in the freezer to really calm them down."

A Balled-up Workout

Amanda inspired me to become a permanent Jazzerciser. A few years later, a new instructor came on board. During our floor work back then we used large rubber balls, which were piled up in a closet for us. But I wanted to be special. I had to have my own.

Off I went with Larry to Sports Authority. The young salesman, looking more like a salesboy with the chubby cheeks of a five-year-old, took us to the back wall where the balls were on display. One was fully inflated as a demo, the rest collapsed in boxes. Showing off, smugly, I chose the largest one, 75-cm (29.53 inches). Baby Face gave me a funny look, but said nothing. Intimidated, I guess, by my aggressive confidence in my choice. We took it home.

So where can you store a ball this size when you're not working out? I stashed it in a corner of the dining room. Mind you, we didn't actually have a free corner. The only one available was already occupied by cartons of our mystery novels for book signings. Nevertheless, I set the ball between two cartons and said, "Stay!"

But exercise balls are social creatures, playful and sensitive. Mine interpreted the corner as a punishment, a Time Out. Its feelings were hurt. Using its bulbous size as leverage, it refused to recognize that I was the grownup. To make its point, it consistently rolled out of the corner to join the family.

Wednesday arrived—a day scheduled for resistance tubes and balls. On this day my ball would make its debut. Finally, I would get to show off my prowess and agility. But in the front hall, I realized I hadn't thought out the logistics. The ball barely fit through our front door. And I could barely get it into the roomy trunk of my Honda SUV. At the church, I carried the ball in both hands up the steps. It took two women to hold the double doors open for me.

Our instructor spotted me and started laughing. Then she whooped and guffawed. "Rosemary," she said, "I'm six-feet and I only use a 65-cm!" Her reaction should've given me a hint.

For our first ball exercise, the idea was to straddle it, feet flat on the floor, and squeeze our legs together to strengthen our adductors, our inner thighs. Thighs, shmighs. With my short legs, I only managed to wedge my knees around the back few inches of the ball. No way could I straddle it.

What happened was this. At Sports Authority I should have taken Baby Face's funny look as a sign. It didn't occur to me to read the dimensions of the ball on the box. After Wednesday's class, I got the box out and read: "For 6'1 and over." I'm five-four. I ended up donating the ball to a physical therapy facility.

More snippets of conversations heard in Severna Park and Honolulu

"My husband's an engineer—you know, everything black and white."

"At my kid's middle school there was a big scandal. Some kids spiked the Sunny Delight with vodka and fifteen kids got expelled. Even if a kid didn't drink it but handed the pitcher to another kid, he was in trouble. They want the kids to learn not get involved. There's a lot of controversy about whether the discipline was appropriate."

"I'm English but my husband and I came to Honolulu years ago and stayed. My father's still in Staffordshire. He's 102 and lives with his girlfriend. She's 90."

"We moved from Korea to Kansas thirty-five years ago. It was nothing but flat and cows. You could drive for eight hours and see nothing but cows. I couldn't stand it. We came to Hawaii."

"I gave my husband your *Cry Ohana* bookmark. He said, 'Buy that book!'"

"Would you like to buy it?" I asked. "I'll autograph it personally to him."

"No."

I kind of avoided her after that. But a few months later, I asked her, "How's your husband?"

"He died."

One of my classmates (years ago) was a kindergarten teacher of ESL (English as a Second Language). She always came to Jazzercise with the latest photos of her fluffy white dog, a Bichon Frise. She told me he wore a sweat suit to bed every night. During the Christmas holidays, she brought him to her ESL class dressed as Santa Paws.

A classmate was complaining about how much work she had to do to prepare Thanksgiving dinner. She had told me her son lived in her building.

"Maybe your son can help you," I said.

"Oh, no. He's a quadriplegic."

I felt bad that I hadn't known.

Larry and I had a supremely gifted friend, Ted Brown, who was a professional classical pianist. Larry asked him, "How can you memorize so many passages that are so difficult?"

"The muscles in my fingers have memory," said Ted.

I've discovered the same thing during Jazzercise. We had a new dance with one arm and one leg extended four times, but I kept bending my right leg and bringing it up to my waist. Then I realized, *Oops! That's not what Caroline is doing. This is a new dance.* My muscles were remembering a previous routine. It's a lesson. I have to concentrate, focus, and pay attention. And that's the whole point. That's how the program keeps us alert and motivated.

Because of COVID, classes are still held only on Zoom. I'm doing that, too. I also acquired an official DVD of a Jazzercise class and often "attend" it in our kitchen. It's all okay, but I miss the togetherness. Before COVID, for over a year our daughter Jackie had routinely attended my class, which delighted me. I would go early to get one of the limited parking spaces, but she always came at least ten minutes late. Once after class she told me, laughing, "I got a great parking space. I got rewarded for my bad behavior."

Four of My Favorite Products

Here are four simple products that are lifesavers for me. All the items are ours; three photos are mine. Larry took my picture.

1. Bed in a Bag. No longer do I need a bedspread—that heavy, clunky thing you have to take off at night and try to fold, or at least scrunch up and find a place for. And then deal with again making the bed in the morning. The comforter is the bedspread and comes with matching sheets, pillow cases, and shams. Sometimes even a bed ruffle. Bed-making time: sixty seconds.

2. The basic steel nutcracker with its two handles. What a blessed gizmo—and I don't even eat nuts. It hurts my hypersensitive hands to open screw-top bottles of water, soda, or diet tonic water. My steel nutcracker only requires one quick turn of the wrist. According to an Internet source, the Greek philosopher Aristotle probably invented the nutcracker, "a pincer-like tool with two levers." Imagine that! There's apparently no limit to Aristotle's 2,000-year impact on humanity.

3. Rubber scraper. So simple, yet the most efficient way to get all the batter, gravy, or pudding out of a bowl or pan. And perfect for licking frosting.

4. Flip-up sunglasses, to clip onto my own glasses when I'm driving. In Honolulu the sun can disappear in a split second, then burst back out two minutes later. And so practical to flip up in parking garages, which are always quite dark. Unless, of course, you're wearing dark glasses to travel incognito.

Dear Readers: If you have a favorite simple gadget, implement, or device (not including lifesavers like dishwashers) you'd like to share, you can email me at **roselarry@magicile.com.**

My Wonderful Hat

I bought the hat at Macy's. Black, with a wide brim that went from ear to ear. It was made of straw so soft that I could fold it in thirds like a business letter and fit it into a compartment of my not-very-large purse.

Most sun hats look stiff, or floppy-goofy, or standard like a baseball cap. This one flattered me. Strangers, even men, complimented me. "Great hat!"

A medical diagnosis compelled me to buy it. During a routine visit to my ophthalmologist, he told me I had the beginnings of cataracts—not unusual for a seventy-year-old.

That didn't satisfy me. "What can I do to slow things down?"

"Always wear sunglasses," he said, "and a hat with a brim."

That did it, I began my quest. It should have been easy. There are a zillion sun hats just begging to be bought. But I had a problem. Every hat I tried on drowned my head. The problem is that I have thin hair. According to my primary care doctor, I have female-pattern baldness. I can't even consider a "fall," one of those cute hair extensions flopping around in a bin at Rite Aid; my hair is too thin to secure it in place. If I were crossing a street and turning my head to check for oncoming cars, the fall would fly off like a bird flapping its wings.

After six months of searching, Macy's in Glen Burnie, Maryland, rescued me with the perfect hat—and it actually fit! It became my trademark. Even near-sighted friends could recognize me a block away. I wore it joyfully for three years.

Then disaster struck. Larry and I were taking our daily walk on the B&A Trail, the marvelous path lined with woods and wildflowers that extends from Annapolis to Baltimore. We walked a mile almost every day even in the rain, but on this day, huge drops began to fall, then a torrent, drenching us during a long stretch of the trail far from our car. To protect my black hat, I took it off and tucked it under my belly pack. It fell on the ground. I stooped to rescue it and again hid it under my belly pack. Thunder forced us to rush to the car, laughing, congratulating ourselves that at least we got our heart-healthy walk in.

The rains and charcoal-gray skies continued for two days. Suddenly, the light dawned—inside my head. I hadn't seen my black hat in the house. I couldn't even remember bringing it in from the car. I searched every inch of my car, then the house from basement to bedrooms, even digging in my laundry hamper. How could this be? Did I drop it on the trail?

We kept up our walks under sunny skies, but I spent most of the time scanning the woods and benches. No sign of my hat.

One afternoon we saw a park employee atop a huge riding mower, clearing out vast swaths of overgrown brush. As we passed a new-mown strip near the parking lot, I saw something familiar. On the ground near a tall juniper, a fragment of black peeked out. I darted over, grabbed it, and pulled—a length of mauled, shredded, soft black straw. The remnants of my beloved hat. I had dropped it in the rain. The riding mower had gotten to it.

Larry summarized the blunt truth. "You were trying to protect it from a little water and, instead, you killed it."

In Judaism, *Kaddish* is the mourner's prayer. Was I allowed to say it over my deceased hat? I hope so, because I did. Let's just say it brought me closure.

Skating on Thin Ice

I went to Cumberland School in Whitefish Bay, Wisconsin, a suburb north of Milwaukee that spread out along Lake Michigan. We lived three blocks from school, which had a green lawn campus so large it held both a football field and separate soccer field. Plus a playground with a jungle gym and monkey bars, both of which I hated. At recess, all the other girls would hang upside down on the monkey bars, their hair flying, their hands trying to hold their skirts around their legs so their panties wouldn't show. I considered the whole activity idiotic—and terrifying. I always ended up isolated, embarrassed while bouncing a ball, the only sissy girl standing next to the teacher-monitor.

Cumberland went from kindergarten to eighth grade, and we had a football team for junior high boys. Eighth grade rescued me. I was a cheerleader and raucously practiced my cheers on the linoleum floor in our kitchen. Fortunately, no tryouts were required. We had more cheerleaders than the team had players—so many of us that we were spread out along the entire length of the field.

Every winter, the football field was flooded for an ice skating rink. This was Wisconsin, with long, often subzero, winters. When I was eight, my parents gave me my first ice skates for Chanukah. Not the double runner kind for little kids, but shoe skates with single blades, the real thing. I took them to school, and when the bell rang at 3:30 I ran to the skating pond. I had never been on skates before. Not ever. The after-school races were already in progress. I sat down on the frozen ground, shoved my feet into the skates, laced them up, and entered a once-around-the-pond race. Skater after skater finished and I was still only halfway around, doggedly pushing myself forward—mostly on my ankles. It didn't occur to me to quit and I was not the least bit embarrassed. When I finally crossed the finish line, I was greeted by a chorus of "Yea!" and mittens clapping.

In eighth grade I'd rush home from school and quickly do my homework so I could go skating after dinner. Those were safer times. In 1948 there was no question about my being allowed to walk three blocks in the dark to school to skate until nine o'clock and then walk home alone.

Feeling quite grownup, we all carried our skates the same way: first tying the laces together, then slinging one skate over the shoulder and one in front. I couldn't wait to get to the rink—I'd made a new friend, a boy named Harry. He was eleven, two years younger than I, in sixth grade. His father, whom I"ll call Mr. Zachary, was my science teacher. Harry was a lanky five foot four, my height, with sensitive chiseled features and warm gray eyes.

We met for the first time in the ice rink Warming House, a sturdy wood shack at one end of the rink. It had a stove in the center and benches along the walls, and smelled of humid air, musty wood, and damp mittens. The sound of skates treading on the bare floor was a muted thud as our blades sank briefly into the soft planks. Harry and I sat next to each other as we put on our skates. As we glided onto the ice, we began chatting, about school, about this and that. Round and round we glided, under the stars, in the cold crisp night. After half an hour, getting cold, we returned to the Warming House to blow our noses and take the chill off as we hovered over the stove. Then back out for more skating—this time holding mittened hands. We continued our skating friendship several times a week. I didn't mind that he was two years younger.

A month later, our friendship burst into icy shards. I was in Mr. Zachary's science class, picking up an assignment from his desk, when his raspy voice caught me by surprise. "Rosemary!"

This did not sound good. I'd always thought of him as a decent teacher, and he gave me pretty good grades. But at times his cruder side escaped when he'd make a joke or remark that was slightly out of place. I stopped short. What could he possibly want? He had gun-gray hair, a heavily lined face, and gray eyes. But where his son's were gentle, Mr. Zachary's had the look of the enemy as they bore into mine. He said, or rather, asked only one sentence:

"Don't you think you're robbing the cradle?"

My insides shriveled. I walked away, to the safe haven of my desk at the back of the room. I knew what he meant and felt a dejection so overwhelming I wanted to cry. Harry and I weren't doing anything wrong. How could he be so mean?

I continued to skate after supper. But Harry didn't. We occasionally passed each other in the hall and waved tentatively. I graduated from eighth grade in June and went off to high school. We never saw each other again. And even today, I still feel a sense of injustice, a sense of loss.

Renoir and Raphael

About fifteen years ago, we were in Washington, D.C. for the day. With us was Nancy Suzuki-Slakter, a close friend visiting from Honolulu. As we drove down Connecticut Avenue, we saw long, narrow banners attached to streetlights high over the road, every two blocks or so. Larry slowed the car to an almost-crawl so we could see what the colorful banners were all about. They bore a detail of Renoir's most famous painting, *Luncheon of the Boating Party*, and the words "I'm back!" in large letters. The painting had been on tour and was now safely ensconced in its permanent home, the venerable Phillips Collection on 21st Street Northwest.

What struck me about the enchanting banner was this. It assumed, correctly, that Washington teems with art lovers. We happened that very day to be headed with Nancy to the Phillips. What luck! Inside, our very first stop was down the stairs to a small gallery paneled in rich dark wood. Months earlier, Larry and I had joined friends in that gallery to hear a piano recital, and the walls had been covered with works by Picasso, Braque, and other timeless artists. Oh, the joy of listening to exquisite music surrounded by those paintings.

Now one paneled wall was devoted exclusively to *Luncheon of the Boating Party*. It hung in all its glory, maybe four feet long and three feet high. The venue of the scene is a restaurant in the French town of Chatou, near Paris. Renoir created a romantic setting for his real-life friends as they enjoyed lunch, wine, and camaraderie on a veranda overlooking the Seine.

A vibrating charisma emanates from the painting; each figure is engaged with others. Renoir's young fiancée is pursing her lips in a kiss for her little terrier sitting on the table in front of her. Seated across from her, in a yellow straw hat, is the Impressionist artist and art patron Gustave Caibotte (whom I had never heard of before). I glanced at the dregs in the bottom of a wine glass, and when I stepped closer, I saw how Renoir had achieved the image with small strokes of gray and white.

The painting glowed with *joie de vivre*. I wanted to be at the party.

Sophomore year at Smith College I took Art 1-1, my first art course, absolutely essential. I would be going to Geneva, Switzerland, for my junior year with the Smith Group. In the lecture hall, professors on stage with pointers discussed huge slides of the world's preeminent art and architecture.

It was in that class that I discovered *The School of Athens* by Renaissance artist Raphael, By the end of the course it was my favorite painting of all time. It gave me chills. It's in the Vatican, one of four monumental works by Raphael. They're frescoes, the art of painting on moist plaster with water-based pigments.

Containing at least thirty dynamic figures, *The School of Athens* symbolizes the unity of art, science, and philosophy, interlaced with the idea of love of learning. The two compelling central figures are Plato and Aristotle. Others include Socrates, Pythagoras, and Ptolemy, The scene throbs with energy and activity, and scholars still speculate on who some of the people are. Raphael did not specifically designate each one.

Junior year, during our spring break from the University of Geneva and the Graduate Institute of International Studies, four of us classmates traveled together to Italy. Of course, in Rome we rushed to the Vatican and beelined to Michelangelo's Sistine Chapel. And then to the Stanza, the four rooms of floor-to-ceiling works by Raphael.

Holding my breath, I was about to view the one painting in the world that I wanted to see more than any other, anywhere. I rushed into the vast room and stood before it—paralyzed with disappointment. *The School of Athens* was covered with scaffolding and protective canvas work cloths. For restoration? Cleaning? I never found out. Bottom line: I could hardly see a thing.

Just a few weeks ago, Larry and I were doing a *New York Times* crossword puzzle at the kitchen table and one of the clues was "Figure in Raphael's *School of Athens*." Six letters and we'd already filled in the last two: "i" and "d."

"Do you think it's Euclid?" I asked Larry.

"Sure," he said, "the Father of Geometry."

"Euclid" was correct in the puzzle, but I didn't remember him being in the painting. So after supper, I researched it online and happily drowned myself in interpretations of all the figures in Raphael's masterpiece.

Sailing—or Not
Tacking between fact and fiction

The plan suddenly made sense. Yes! I had brooded over it for months, my secret plan to divorce my first husband after only one year of marriage. I had even made an appointment with a family-practice lawyer. But then Life kicked me in the butt—or rather, my gut. I got pregnant and shelved the plan—as well as my common sense.

I should have known from the start that this was another of my husband's really bad ideas. Marvin wanted a sailboat. He had read every book in existence about he-men like Joshua Slocum, who single-handed a sailboat around the world. Marvin ached to be one of them.

We had just moved from Yonkers in northern Manhattan to Maryland for his new job with the Federal Government and settled into an obscure community near Annapolis called Stillwater Estates. The little suburb was one of many crowded between two rivers, the Severn and the Magothy, both feeding into the Chesapeake Bay. I never liked the name "Magothy"; it sounded too much like "maggots."

Stillwater Estates was a place that time forgot. The largest store was Pantry Pride, from which I once bought a Boston cream pie, apparently not fresh, and threw up for two hours.

We had moved there to be near the water—to fulfill Marvin's dream. The trouble was, he had never sailed anything except his toy boat in the bathtub. He'd never even set foot on a sailboat. He grew up a Jewish boy in a congested neighborhood of Chicago. When I married this pudgy guy with dark, curly hair, I was naïve, in denial about his true personality. He was high-strung, a glaring red flag for any sailor's temperament. Still, he had that yearning and frustration.

Adding to his discontent, my husband, Marvin Maurice Goldberg, hated his name. He longed to have one that reflected his macho alter ego. Preferably a herky name like actors Rip Torn or Vin Diesel. He swore that when he did his round-the-world sail he'd write a book about it and use a pen name worthy of him. I could see it now. Bull Biceps Goldberg.

On weekends we went sightseeing in Washington, D.C. only an hour away. On one particular Saturday, Marvin kept driving—into Virginia, to Mount Vernon. *How thrilling*, I thought, *I've never been there.* After ending our tour at George Washington's slave quarters, Marvin laid it on me that he knew about a large marina nearby on the Potomac River. Now I got it. The sightseeing was just a pretext to check it out. We strolled down to the docks, when a tall, thin man with wire-rimmed glasses confronted us. *David Niven,* I thought, the imperious British actor reincarnated.

"Yes?" he asked, his clipped mustache bobbing up and down already in disapproval. "May I help you?"

Marvin cleared his throat. "Uh, yeah, we're planning on buying a sailboat and we wondered if we could dock it here."

"What size did you have in mind?"

"Eighteen feet, I guess. Around there."

David Niven's lips curled up at the corners in a forced almost-smile. "I don't think so," he sniffed. "We repair and moor presidential yachts."

Marvin and I slunk away. A week later he slightly altered his dream. He'd found an ad for a twenty-foot power boat—motor *not* included—that "needs a little work, a great bargain at $100."

Now this was 1968. Today that would translate to $1,000. Maybe more. The minute Marvin saw it he fell in love. And I fell in love with wishing I hadn't married him. The boat was a behemoth, a huge tub with about a dozen layers of paint, all visible, all chipped, curled up, and faded. You could see its history like rings on a tree. Had Washington crossed the Delaware in it?

We were in an early stage of marriage. When Marvin said "Take your checkbook" I obediently did, thus leaving myself no excuse like, "Sorry, dear, I forgot it. Guess we can't do this." Timidly, I asked, "Does it leak?"

"Only a little," the owner mumbled, refusing to look me in the eye. "A few new planks should take care of it."

Great, I thought. Marvin had never so much as picked up a screwdriver. "Flathead? Phillips? Are those cartoon characters?"

Three days later we took delivery on the tub. I stared out the living room window and gasped. In our driveway, it looked like an obese Noah's Ark. On its trailer the tub bulged out sideways onto our lawn, casting a giant shadow that would replace any blades of grass trying desperately to grow. We would need to leave our cars on the street until Marvin could get the boat into seaworthy shape. Maybe in ten years. More likely, never.

Marvin visited every marine supply store in Annapolis, actng like he fit into the seadog scene, and discovered that marine paint did not exactly cost the same as a gallon of exterior Sears paint. He shrugged. "We'll just eat hot dogs more often."

Oh, sure, I thought. *Like we'd been dining on pheasant under glass and beef Wellington every night.*

We were munching on our Sunday bagels when the doorbell rang. Two men in creased chinos and polo shirts stood on the porch. Were they the Bobbsey twins of Stillwater Estates?

"Hi, I'm Dan Fallworth, our community association president, and this here is Hank Seitz, vice president. We know you're new to the community. Welcome, by the way. But unfortunately there's a problem that we need to bring to your attention." His boardroom voice didn't sound welcoming at all. Without an invitation, they barreled through the door and into our living room, seating themselves as if they were our best friends.

"What seems to be the problem?" Marvin asked.

"It's your boat," Dan said. No pleasant sidling into the subject.

Marvin piped up brightly. "Yeah, it's gonna be great when we get it all fixed up and—"

"That's just it," Dan interrupted. "You can't do repairs to it here."

Marvin sputtered, "Uh, you mean in the driveway? We can probably get it into the backyard. Of course, we'll have to take down the chain-link fence, but we'll put it back up as soon as it's ready to be moved to a marina and—"

Hank stopped him cold. "No, Marvin, you don't understand. You're not allowed to do boat repairs or even car repairs here in Stillwater Estates. Not in your own driveway. Not even in your own backyard."

"Why not?" Marvin asked, pulling a cigarette pack out of his shirt pocket. He lit up his fifth or sixth smoke of the day.

Dan frowned, his bushy, black eyebrows turning into a single-line like a fuzzy caterpillar. "Well, it's like this, Marvin. Our community covenants and restrictions forbid it. For all of us."

"Community covenants? Restrictions?" Marvin's voice squeaked. "Nobody ever told *us* about them."

Oy vey! A faint memory of those documents hovered in the nether region of my brain. I remembered not reading them, just stuffing them in a folder as if they didn't apply to us. After all, we'd been New Yorkers renting a fourth-floor walkup. What did we know about such rules?

Hank abruptly stood and crossed his arms over his chest. "Surely," he began with the soft, understanding voice of a prison guard, "you asked your real estate agent to provide you with a copy of the documents. No self-respecting home buyer would ignore such essential information. You have one week to get rid of that eyesore in your driveway."

"Or what?" Marvin and I asked in unison.

The neighborhood Gestapo left without another word. We sold our decrepit Noah's Ark for practically zilch. So much for my husband's fantasy of even motor-boating single-handed around the world. I assumed this costly debacle had convinced him that his obsession was reckless and irresponsible. Boy, was I wrong.

A year later, I was six months pregnant. Marvin discovered an ad in our hometown newspaper for a sailboat: twenty footer, bargain-priced, docked just a few miles away on the Magothy River. After supper, when I was ready to put my feet up and commune with the miniature baby kicking joyfully in my belly, Marvin announced that Butch, the owner of this craft, would take us out for a sunset sail in half an hour.

The boat was docked at the end of a pier. Butch opened the hatch and pointed to the sleeping quarters down below: two short, pencil-thin bunks that might have been cozy for Tiny Tim. We sailed in a light breeze for a few minutes, close to shore, with Butch shouting instructions to Marvin. His most frequent advice: "If what you're doing doesn't work, do the opposite."

Huh? "Butch," I said, politely, "I need to use your bathroom."

"It's called the head," he muttered. "We don't have one. We use a bucket."

"Maybe *you* use a bucket," I snapped. "Marvin! I need to go home. Now!"

Before he could even respond, the sailboat jolted forward, *thunk, thunk, thud,* and lurched to a halt. "I'll be damned," Butch said, "we've run aground."

Our sunset sail had ended. Darkness descended. We now had only a half-moon to guide us. Marvin tried to hide his annoyance. "I thought you knew these waters."

"Well, uh, my wife and I just moved here a month ago."

"Where from?" Marvin asked.

"Kansas. The boat came with the house. I've only had 'er out once."

Wonderful. It was then that I learned a new word: kedging. Butch dug through a storage cabinet in the stern and hauled out a small anchor attached to a long rope. "This'll do it," he said. He threw the anchor out about ten feet. It plopped into the water. "Kedging works great," he said. "What happens is, the anchor hooks into the mud and sand. I pull on the rope and free the boat. It'll get us outta here."

He pulled and grunted. We sat and sat, my bladder near bursting. The kedging didn't work. But something else did. The tide started coming in. The boat lifted up just a fraction and began to float. Hooray! But then a fresh problem caught us. The wind had decided to take a nap; we were becalmed. "Good thing I installed this outboard motor," Butch said with strained cheeriness. He yanked on the string, again and again. Finally the engine caught and we putt-putted along.

"Is this eggbeater ever going to get us there?" I whined.

Our host looked crushed. At the dock, the two men helped me out, but Butch kept Marvin on the boat, still pathetically continuing his sales pitch, followed by instructions on how to lower sails and make the craft shipshape. I silently stole away, ten or fifteen feet along the narrow sandy beach. In the dark, near a shadowed clump of mangroves, I lowered my bulky self onto the sand and stretched my legs out primly in front of me. Carefully, I hiked up my maternity dress, fluffed the skirt out of harm's way—and peed.

Marvin did not make an offer on the boat. Even he was disillusioned.

My seventh month and I had already ballooned. Marvin seemed not to notice. Still pursuing his dream, he discovered another ad, this one in the *Washington Post.* "Not again," I wailed. The ad hawked the Klepper Boat, "for the sailor on a budget." Pregnancy had obviously clouded my judgment and resolve. We drove to D.C. to check it out.

When we arrived, I expected a large, inviting showroom with bright lights, pretty boats, and salesmen in navy blazers with gold buttons. The lone salesman had slicked-back hair, wore a faded windbreaker, and had a nametag: Oliver. His domain was a single room containing two steel desks with swivel chairs, a few file cabinets, and a coffeemaker on the counter. My first thought was, *This furniture is hot, stolen from heaven knows where. It just came off a panel truck heading down I-95. Where is the showroom?* Oliver led us downstairs into the basement. And behold! There on the floor sat a gray rubber canoe. Fitted out in the bow was a vertical stick, "the mast," as Oily Oliver called it. It had a triangular sail attached.

"The advantage to this awesome craft," he bragged, "is that it's inflatable! And it comes with paddles if you're just going canoeing. You can take this baby anywhere, deflated in your trunk, and just pump it up. It's a breeze," he laughed, "if you'll excuse the pun."

Several hundred dollars poorer, on a chilly Sunday morning, we drove fifteen miles down to the South River. We found a patch of beach that didn't look private to set up our Klepper. But that was our last shred of good luck that day. Oily Oliver had lied. The little pump proved not to be a breeze. It took forty-five minutes to inflate, with Marvin sweating and swearing. If curses were tornadoes, we'd have been in the eye of the storm. Finally, our Klepper puffed up to its full glory. Marvin propped up the mast with the sail "rigged" to it (in proper lingo) and dragged the canoe to the water's edge. I lowered myself heavily into the bow, Marvin climbed into the stern and we set sail. Sort of. Our craft sat lower in the water than I'd expected, with my belly higher than the gunnels, making me feel extra vulnerable. I wanted to be home, safe on the couch, reading the Sunday funnies. By now, the South River was populated with sailboats, kayaks, and motor boats. We bobbed and splashed as the wakes of the other boats tossed us about. But for a few minutes our little sail actually propelled us forward.

Suddenly, the light breeze turned brisk, then instantly into aggressive gusts. And the worst happened. The bow of our rubber canoe folded over, to the left, taking the puny stick of a mast and the sail straight down with it. The mast hit the gunnel and the sail flopped into the South River. Our rig now lay parallel to the water in humiliating defeat. The reason was obvious: the mast was improperly designed. It had never been "seated" in a wooden structure that would have kept it upright. The inventor of this wretched Klepper had never heard of wind!

Experienced boaters passed us slowly, looking curious and baffled. An old salt on his forty-footer snickered. Several kind people called out, "Would you like some help?" Meaning, want a tow? Marvin bravely waved back, "No, thanks." He began paddling. I paddled, too, but laboriously. Somehow we made it back to the tiny beach. We climbed out, and Marvin stomped around, breathing fire. I expected him to deflate the canoe and stash it in our trunk. Oh, no. He'd had it. He grabbed my hand and trudged through the sand toward our car. "Don't even look back," he growled, like Lot telling his wife as they fled from Sodom. "Forget the damned thing."

I often wonder what happened to it. At first I romantically thought it would float back into the water, sink, and become known to the locals as the Klepper Coral Reef. Then I remembered: coral does not grow on rubber, or any other soft surface. Well, then, maybe kids are playing in it, enjoying the free canoe. That would be the next best thing.

Our baby boy was born, and nine years later, Marvin and I divorced. My loving, sensible second husband is a Navy veteran, who logged over a hundred-thousand miles at sea during the Korean War. No way would he own a boat.

"Sailing—or Not" won writing awards from the National League of American Pen Women/Honolulu Branch and the Writers' Workshop of Asheville, North Carolina.

King Tut Returns

He sat on the mahogany end table, presiding over our living room, a furry sphinx of orange marmalade and vanilla. He could have fooled a visitor: he looked like the final accessory the decorator had set down. Seated on his haunches, silent and still as the pyramids, his amber eyes glinted with ancient wisdom. You see, our cat was King Tut reincarnated.

Hoppy. Such a plebeian, philistine name, yet quite understandable, considering his animal shelter origin. Those blessed workers simply don't have time to conjure up monikers like Amenhotep and Ptolemy. Besides, how could they have known this kitten was King Tut? But my daughter, Miriam, and I knew. From the moment he padded across our threshold, we recognized the noble carriage, the youthful exuberance, the ruling fervor.

But no surprises there. Over 5,000 years ago in Egypt, cats came to be worshiped and loved by both royalty and the populace. Unearthed tombs contain wondrous images of cats: wall paintings, sculpture, jewelry, and amulets. The feline deity Bastet became a household goddess, often guarding doorways to ward off evil spirits. This national reverence began when cats proved to be excellent hunters of grain-eating rodents.

What was King Tut doing in *our* house, anyway? Since the discovery of his tomb in the early 1920s, archaeologists have been analyzing his mummified remains—and quarreling over their significance. He probably got fed up. So he traded the riches that accompanied him to the Hereafter for our Sears oriental rugs and Goodwill buffet.

As the sun god Ra ascended to the hour of 7:00 a.m., Hoppy plotted his day. His right ear twitched as he heard Miriam's chair pull up to the kitchen table. He slipped off the sofa, each muscle of his body following the other like a Slinky descending the stairs. Out of the corner of one glowing eye, he studied me. Pretending to head nowhere, he ambled toward the kitchen and settled himself into the corner behind Miriam's chair. His eyelids closed—as heavily and inexorably as the door to Aida's tomb. He then raised and lowered each paw as if preparing for a long sleep.

But it was a ruse. As my daughter reached for her glass of milk, Hoppy sprang toward her plate. With one swipe, his teeth clamped down on half of her toasted, cream-cheesed bagel. And off he raced to the living room to consume his treasure under our only antique chair. Miriam, laughing too hard and too long to gobble up the other half, ran for the school bus. Never mind that she was hungry. Hoppy could do no wrong.

About that chair. It was square, with ornately carved wood, upholstered in vibrant blue velvet. The very moment I brought it home and set it under a window, Hoppy streaked across the room and leapt into it, claiming it as his. Have you ever seen ancient Egyptian art? Azure blue appears as a dominant color, symbolic of life and the Nile River itself. Sometimes pharaohs are even depicted with blue faces. (Hoppy the aristocrat would thoughtfully consume a bagel—or fresh live mouse—*under* the sacred chair, not in it.)

One morning, I sat at my desk paying bills. A quiet hour passed without incident. Suddenly, I heard a tap-tap-tap, soft as a camel's hoofs on desert sands. I stole down the carpeted stairs and peered around the corner into the kitchen. Hoppy lay on the vinyl floor, stretched out on his right side. His left paw gently tap-tap-tapped the corner of the fridge door as he tried to lure it open. The paw increased its momentum. One final pull and the door swung wide.

With the grace of Cleopatra's barge gliding down the Nile, Hoppy rose on his hind legs. Anchoring one front paw firmly to a metal rack, he coaxed out a single can of Bud Light. And why not? Beer prevailed as the favorite beverage for centuries in ancient Egypt. Legend has it that Osiris, god of the Underworld, taught humans to make beer. The Bud Light landed upright on the floor. Hoppy sniffed his booty, no doubt wondering, *How do you open this newfangled thing?* Disappointed, he sauntered off to his blue velvet throne to dream of a more succulent treat: a Red Sea Bass, perhaps.

I, on the other hand, had to call in a General Electric technician. For numerous *piastres*, he placed wood blocks under the front corners of the fridge, thereby shifting the door's weight against our twelve-pound marauder.

The SPCA had assured us Hoppy was an indoor kitten. "He's never been outside," they said. "He'll never want to go out." Wrong! He spent much of his day lurking near our front door, knowing that, sooner or later, it would open so he could escape for a few hours. The Front Door Wars turned into a battle of wits—which my daughter and I usually lost. I can only conclude that King Tut inherited an alley cat gene.

Our furry pharaoh reigned uncontested over our family for thirteen years. My grieving imagination runs wild as I sight Hoppy look-alikes everywhere. Holding court in a Baltimore bookshop. On my own street, peering out the bay window of a neighbor's house. In a kitty litter commercial (how demeaning!).

I still grieve for Hoppy thirty years later. Nevertheless, today I might be heading to the SPCA for a new rescue cat—maybe a female this time. A queen would be nice. (Yes, I know, I'm getting greedy.) Who will it be? Nefertiti? Or Liliuokolani, last ruler of the Hawaiian monarchy? I have so much to look forward to.

Stumbling in the Shadow of the Pyramids

My parents didn't give me a middle name. When I asked my mother why, she told me "Rosemary" was long enough. But her reasoning left me disgruntled, as if an essential part of me were missing. At age fourteen, after reading *Gone with the Wind* and *Forever Amber*, I made a declaration at the dinner table.

"I've decided to give myself a middle name. My first choice is Scarlett, but I'll settle for Amber."

"Jewish girls aren't called Scarlett or Amber," Mother said. "Now please clear the table."

Despite my disappointment, I stubbornly daydreamed that I was destined for great things. "Things" have bombarded me my whole life, but not always what I had in mind—especially not on a tour of Egypt. It was 2008, years before the current political turmoil. Everyone else on our tour was discovering Abu Simbel with its four statues of Ramses II seated in mammoth stone chairs; and the leonine crumbling Sphinx with its human face. Me? I was discovering that I'm accident-prone.

My accident-proneness just couldn't wait 'til I got home. It couldn't allow me two stress-free weeks to visit a country I'd never set foot in again. No, indeed. It had to make my acquaintance in Cairo.

It was our first morning and I was about to have my first catastrophe. All because of my innocent little travel alarm. It was the reliable wind-up kind. But Larry hated it; it rang with a grating jangle.

"It's supposed to," I told him. "That way we won't miss the bus." He also hated it because it ticked—aggressively. He insisted I put it on the desk across the room so he wouldn't hear the ticking. So that morning, at 5:30 when the alarm rang, my spouse growled, "Get that thing!" I jerked my jet-lagged body out of bed and stumbled to the desk to shut it off. But my bare foot met the desk chair, swelling my big toe and turning it azure blue—symbolic of life and the Nile itself. Lucky me.

129

Mother used to tell me stories about Naughty Nancy and Goody Two-shoes—a poorly disguised sermon. Well, no more Goody Two-shoes for me. The rest of our trip I would let that vicious little alarm just ring itself out.

I make a studied effort not to limp and told no one about my toe. Who would want to hear? We were on our way to the Pyramids with our guide, a pleasant, scholarly fellow, fortyish, named Mahmoud. To pronounce his name correctly, you had to say it like Mach-mood.

On the bus, a stranger accompanied us: a dark-haired olive-skinned young man, who sat directly behind the driver in the aisle seat. Wearing a black suit, white shirt, and subdued narrow tie, he was our tour's personal guard, a member of Egypt's Tourist Police. Although his weapon wasn't visible, he was armed. He would be with us for our entire tour. *Is this good or bad?* I wondered. In 2005, Egypt experienced a rash of terrorist attacks on tourists. I guess I should have felt comforted.

I assumed that the Pyramids on the Giza plateau were located miles from civilization, majestically set in the pristine desert as shown in photographs. Not quite. They're situated on the immediate outskirts of Cairo. Our bus chugged slowly through a neighborhood of dilapidated houses. Dust filled the air, rising from the baked, crumbling streets. A narrow canal ran down the center of the road. A local woman carrying a large plastic bag crossed the street and approached the canal. She wore a burka, a full black garment and headdress that exposed only the eyes, hands, and feet. Upending the bag, she tossed its contents—garbage—into the canal. What was that furry object floating just under the surface? Mahmoud said, "It's not uncommon for folks to throw in a dead animal, like a dog or even a cow." A few feet away, small children splashed about in the filthy brown water.

Peering between the sad stucco houses, we saw the Pyramids! The awe-inspiring Great Pyramid, built as a tomb for Pharaoh Khufu, looked different up close. We could see how it was constructed of huge individual stones, more than two million of them.

The next morning we headed to the Egyptian Museum. Mahmoud took us early to avoid the crowds. But lunchtime crept up on us. In the gallery that housed King Tut, our group lined up politely to approach the glass case. Larry leaned on his cane. He wasn't accident-prone; his back just refused to behave. Suddenly, we had company: mobs of newly arrived tourists. Obsessed humanity swarmed toward us. A withered little woman grabbed Larry's cane so she could squeeze in front of him. He yanked it back and recovered his balance. Somehow we made it to poor King Tut.

British Egyptologist Howard Carter discovered Tut's tomb in Egypt's Valley of the Kings in 1922. Carter decided to remove the mummified remains and examine the body itself. But the ingenious royal mummification process involved secure wrappings of gum-coated linen bandages. Carter placed King Tut outside in the sun, hoping to melt the adhesive bindings. They didn't. Carter kept tugging on the bandages anyway. What a disaster. After his debacle, other Egyptologists, for decades, poked at and quarreled over the remains. King Tut's blackened, shriveled body now lay broken in fifty pieces.

We marched back to our bus. As I lowered myself into my seat and turned to look out the window, my right thigh muscle wrenched and spasmed. *Aaah!* Caused by nothing. I had no excuse. I couldn't report that I was straining toward the finish line in a 10-K run for breast cancer research; or cramping up in the two-mile swim during an Ironman Triathlon. I pressed my grimacing lips together and told no one.

We pulled up at the Khan el-Khalili bazaar, Cairo's famed *souk* that dates back to 1382. The "cousins" were waiting for us. Mahmoud, with his subtle wit, called all vendors "cousins." They hovered about us at every site like mosquitoes in a swamp, shoving their postcards, trinkets, and silk scarves in our faces. They understood "No," but it didn't apply to them. They kept pushing, pressing, harassing. I said "No thank you" to one large man, and he shouted, "Okay, g'bye!" and slapped his hand against my shirt sleeve. It was more like a flick of a finger, but the insult stung.

The bazaar contained walls and walls of lovely creations. Larry and I wanted to shop leisurely, but the cousins soured us. Lurking beneath their surface we sensed—I can't seem to find a polite word—hostility. We didn't buy a thing.

Our tour took us outside of Cairo. As we approached the unfathomable expanse of the Sahara, the bus stopped. We were then greeted by a jeep containing four Tourist Police Officers, who became our escorts to every outlying site. That day it was the Step Pyramid at Sakkara. An engineering marvel predating the Great Pyramid, Sakkara is a necropolis, a burial ground for Old Kingdom royalty. Mahmoud led us on a hike around the entire perimeter. I kept my head down, eyes glued to my feet as we churned and stumbled through shifting sands and mounds of gravel. Larry and I stopped for a moment, our chests heaving as the hundred-degree heat filled our lungs. I gazed about to the higher dunes and discovered our four police officers patrolling, their automatic weapons at the ready, protecting us.

We visited a Nubian village. Nubia was the ancient civilization on the southern border of Egypt. At a local home, the hosts invited us to hold the family's pet crocodile—a young female about eighteen inches long, with her fearsome jaws shut tight in a round red clamp. Each member of our tour group came forward for the experience and learned where to grip the animal: placing one hand over the body and the other near the tail. Everyone came forward—except me. I have hypersensitive skin. I worried that the croc's hide would be sharp and scaly and hurt my fingers. When it was almost time to leave, everyone done holding, I changed my mind, rushed forward, and reached out for her.

Taking the little crocodile in my hands, I had a surprisingly tender reaction. Her silvery hide felt soft. Her tiny belly heaved in and out as she breathed. She opened her eyes wide and they glowed a lovely amber-hazel. Knowing I was protected from her dangerous teeth, I had this sense that I held a fragile life.

Back at our hotel in Cairo, the farewell dinner was to start in half an hour. We were leaving for home the next morning. Larry was dressed and waiting patiently for me. I was late. In the shower I began composing a poem for Mahmoud. Wrapping my dripping body in a towel, I sat down at the desk to scribble the verses on a sheet of stationery before they escaped from my head.

Ten minutes to get to the banquet. I put on my bronze-colored blouse flecked with gold threads and the gold dangle earrings we bought in Hong Kong. They were inset with Chinese characters signifying good luck. At least, that's what the salesgirl told us. For all I know, they could have said Kwan's Noodle Shop. Clutching my poem, I strode toward the door, my husband behind me.

Suddenly, I was no longer standing. The floor roses up to meet me. *Slam!* I was lying face down on the floor. Larry rushed to help me. I stared at the underside of my right forearm. A long flap of ripped flesh hung loose, bleeding, scraped by the industrial grade carpet.

Larry leaned over me, his face fraught with anxiety. He lifted me upright. I slipped out of his arms and marched robot-like into the bathroom, digging around in my cosmetic kit for Band-Aids. It took three, side by side, to cover the wound.

"I'm fine!" I chirped, holding up my bandaged arm. "Good as new."

Larry's large hands gently encircled my waist. He studied my face. "Are you really all right? Do you want to forget the dinner and stay up here?"

"Absolutely not," I retorted. "I have my poem to read. I've even rehearsed it."

He looked skeptical. "When I saw you fall, my heart dropped to my toes. Your head came within an inch of that dresser."

Oh boy, that was not good. My husband has a heart condition. The dresser top was solid granite. How could I have been so clumsy?

We managed to arrive on time. I read my poem to enthusiastic applause. We ended the evening with hugs, photos, and promises to keep in touch.

At 5:00 a.m, *jangle jangle jangle.* I let the alarm ring itself into oblivion. We rolled out of bed, drugged with exhaustion and antiquities overload. We had exactly ninety minutes to finish packing, eat breakfast, and be in the lobby for the shuttle that would take us to the airport. Nonstop on Egypt Air to JFK.

I set my suitcase on top of an armchair, balancing it on the two *faux*-Chippendale wooden arms. Only one more thing to stuff in, my sleep shirt. Leaning forward to tuck it into a corner, the suitcase slid askew. I tried to catch it, but my knees buckled under me. *Bam!* I landed on the floor hard on my bottom. A lightning bolt of pain shot through my vertebrae. My *tush* felt like it was welded to the rug. *Crash!* The round end table next to the chair teetered and fell with a great thud. I gazed at it in horror.

"Larry! Did I break the glass?"

"No. It's fine."

In disbelief, I looked again. The beveled circle of heavy glass that had covered the table was lying on the floor, intact.

"But you? Are *you* okay?" he asked.

"No," I whispered. "I can't get up." My strong husband placed his hands in my armpits, lifted me up, and slowly guided me to the bed.

I sank down—and launched into a crying jag because I realized I was so out of control. Egypt's security measures, no matter how elaborate, could not protect me from myself.

We were too late for breakfast. Larry collected the clothes that fell out of my suitcase and did all my last-second stuffing, zipping, and lifting. We were ready to wheel our luggage into the hall. It was now daylight, so before exiting the room, he pulled open the drapes that covered the floor-to-ceiling window. We anticipated a garden view, but instead, our eyes zeroed in on the glass just above the bottom of the window. What we saw was a hole the size of a dime with spider-web cracks emanating from it.

"Oh my God, Larry, did I do that when I fell?"

"No way! You didn't fall anywhere near it." He knelt down and pointed to the hole. "Know what this is? It's a bullet hole. A large caliber."

I gasped. "A bullet hole? But..." I sputtered. "Did it happen while we've had this room?"

"It doesn't look new," Larry said. "But one thing's for sure. The shot came from outside."

We whispered about what to do next. Call hotel management? Yikes! Maybe they knew about the hole, but hadn't gotten around to fixing it. Or maybe they'd call the police, who would want answers and haul us to the station. We'd miss our flight home. We pulled the drapes closed, grabbed our bags, and fled the room. That is, in my heart I fled. Actually, I hobbled.

* * * *

We arrived safely home in Severna Park. Three months later, a Verizon technician was installing FIOS, a fiber-optic system for our TV. Striding through our living room in his work boots and jeans, he stopped in front of the couch and pointed to my newest pillow; I had bought it in the gift shop on our cruise of the Nile.

"I went to Egypt," he said. "That's the Eye of Horus—and you've got it upside down!"

Oops! Mightily embarrassed but grateful, I thanked him and rearranged the pillow.

Poor misunderstood Horus. He's the falcon-headed Egyptian god of light, son of Osiris and Isis. Now that the pillow was right-side-up, what a relief for both of us. All those months I thought he was leering at me.

The Eye of Horus

135

Trapped!
A mind game

I'm upstairs, alone and divorced, in my home office in Chesapeake Shores, a treeless tract in a Maryland suburb. Suddenly, I heard noise downstairs, someone thumping on the front door. It's opening! Heavy shuffling footsteps. Oh my God. Has someone come to rob me? Rape me? Kill me? I instantly make a plan. I'll lock the office door. But the lock is flimsy, a button in the doorknob. I'll move the bookcase against the door. But am I crazy? It's seven feet tall and contains 200 books. If the intruder comes up the stairs, what can I attack him with? Phooey! My can of Raid is under the kitchen sink. I know. I'll squirt him in the eyes with Elmer's Glue. Oh, crap, it won't come out of the bottle fast enough. Better still, the bag of bungee cords on the shelf. I can strangle him. Should I use a red one? Or yellow? But what if he has a gun? I'm doomed.

"Ma'am?" A male voice calls from downstairs.

I open the door an inch. "What? Who's there?"

"ShopExpress, ma'am. Your doorbell didn't work and the front door was open. I need your signature for this package."

"Oh." But is he really ShopExpress? Or just trying to lure me downstairs? My knees wobble as I sidle out of the office and gaze down into the front hall. A stout man stands there. He's stuffed into shorts and polo shirt and wearing a ShopExpress cap. I crouch down to look outside. The company truck is at the curb. But what if he stole the truck and bought his uniform online? He's holding a box in front of him. Does it contain a bomb? Does he plan to get my signature, hand me the box, and bolt out the door before it explodes? But I didn't order anything. I slouch down the stairs. My fingers tremble as I sign the electronic pad.

Mr. Chubby hands me the box, sets a little plastic baggie on top, and dashes out to his truck. I carry them to the picnic table out on the patio. Cold sweat trickles down my armpits under my sweater. Do I dare open the packages? Curiosity overcomes my anguish. With a manicured nail I slice open the box.

There lies a plush red blanket, courtesy of Maryland Public Television, rewarding me for becoming a subscriber. My heart continues a war dance as I open the plastic baggie. Inside I find chocolate kisses wrapped in orange foil. But wait! Is each alluring morsel filled with arsenic? Or strychnine? I'm a chocoholic and decide then and there that if I'm to die, at least I'll die chomping on my favorite food. I unwrap the foil, slowly place a kiss on my tongue, and let it melt. I swallow. I'm still here!

And then I see the tag attached to the baggie: "From Your Friendly ShopExpress Guy, Happy Halloween!"

Why the (Former) Redskins Are Always Winners —No Matter What

This is not easy. I've been a Washington football fan for thirty years and the rumblings have finally turned into reality. The team is no longer allowed to use the name Redskins. I published this essay as a joyous Redskins fan in *Washington Woman* (Oct./Nov. 1995). Reluctantly, I have made the adjustment in the team name. But it's no fun because they haven't chosen a new name yet. So what would be a good choice? How about an animal like so many NFL teams? The Llamas? No, the Dalai Lama would be upset. The Ferrets? Too sneaky. How about a bird? The Robins? Too tame. So I'll just leave it to the experts and hope they don't take forever.

I was a late bloomer as a Washington fan. I lived in Severna Park for two decades before I fell under their spell. But now my love affair with the team is eternal. There's something about the team, even at its down-and-outest, that inspires me to unshakable loyalty.

For much of my adult life I had little interest in football.

Neither college football nor the NFL could compete with the romance of the game as I remembered it in high school in the early Fifties. At Whitefish Bay High I took our school's football games seriously. For an hour before each game, I sold programs at five cents apiece, always selling out quickly, my excitement transmitting itself to every fan entering our little stadium. As I bounced into my seat among my friends, I never ceased to be captivated by the players' sexy uniforms—the tight pants that outlined the boys' cute bottoms and strong, muscled thighs, the huge padded shoulders that radiated masculinity.

Our team was a winner, week after week. The quarterback played brilliantly; I felt faint just watching him trot out onto the field. But what enhanced his standing with me even more was that he sat next to me in Latin class and he was a straight-A student! I barely had the courage to say hello to him. How wonderful could one person be?

After fifteen straight wins, Whitefish Bay lost to South Milwaukee High. We sat silent in the bleachers in disbelief, already grieving. Their team's cheerleaders came over to our side at the close of the game, not with cheers but with jeers. We were a middle-class community and they were a blue-collar town near the breweries. Reveling in their moment of triumph, their resentment of us was almost palpable.

But my life marched on after high school. As I boarded the train for my freshman year at Smith College in Northampton, Massachusetts, I fantasized. I wondered if I could lose enough weight to attract a date for an invitation to the Harvard-Yale game. And glory of glories, I succeeded, not in losing weight, but in getting asked to the game. The best part was phoning my parents about it so Mother could tell all her friends. The worst part was actually attending.

The Yale Bowl teemed with couples in the throes of romance; my date and I weren't one of them. I had met my Yalie date at a freshman mixer and when he called to invite me to the game, I was so eager to accept that I forgot what he actually looked like.

He was a head shorter than I, at least forty pounds lighter, and looked about twelve years old. So I just sat back in my camel's hair coat, determined to throw myself into the thrill of the game. But in 1953 there didn't seem to be any thrill in Ivy League football. There was hardly any cheering. Apparently, it wasn't cool. I have no idea who won. My date fizzled and so did my interest in football—for three decades.

In November, 1986, I had just started dating Larry. On our third date he invited me to a Washington Redskins game. Half-heartedly, I said yes. I had no idea there was a ten-year waiting list for season tickets. But when Larry rang my doorbell that Sunday morning, he was holding a gift for me: a corsage of pom-pom mums in burgundy and gold, the team colors. *Hmm*, I thought, *something important is happening here. This is going to be a near-religious experience.* Well, it wasn't quite that, but it was close. I became an obsessed fan.

Everything I've ever learned about the game I learned from Larry—which was pleasant, because my football education had an ugly beginning. In my third-grade gym class, we were required to play football. The gym teacher had a palsied hand and club foot. Perhaps his frustration over his physical limits led him to compensate by hollering at us eight-year-olds. His thunderous instructions scared me so badly I couldn't concentrate. I just couldn't figure out how this game was played. I complained to my mother, and she came to my rescue.

"Your team has four chances to make ten yards," she said. "Each chance is called a down." Why couldn't my gym teacher explain it that simply? Fate mercifully intervened. The very next week I fell off my bike and broke my wrist. The pain of the compound fracture was nothing compared to my joy at being excused from gym class and football for the rest of the season. I was on Injured Reserves!

Washington was the only team I rooted for in the NFL and I welcomed Larry's commentary. I learned about the nickel defense and onside kicks, double coverage, and third-and-long passing situations. Even Joe Gibbs appealed to me, with his scholarly, gentle look—not your typical head coach.

But in December 1988, a catastrophic event, a tragedy that would change our lives forever, befell our family. I lost my daughter, Miriam Luby Wolfe, on Pan Am Flight 103, the plane destroyed by a terrorist bomb over Lockerbie, Scotland. During the months following the death of my only child, my grief took complex twists. Memories and reminders choked me. I couldn't bear to go to the movies. I couldn't read books about mothers and daughters. Even TV commercials about cheery moms and their kids upset me.

Then September arrived—and with it the NFL's new season. I found, to my surprise, that I was ready for the Redskins. The team provided a welcome distraction because the games took me out of my own reality. For three hours I could focus on this fantasy world instead of on how much I missed Miriam. This world was built on conflict that had nothing to do with me, had nothing to do with girls and their mothers.

As a bonus, in 1991 the Redskins were a hot team. The offensive line of 300-pounders was affectionately called The Hogs. The little clutch of receivers known as The Posse was a combine to be feared. As the season heightened to a frenzy, I also began watching other NFL teams. On Sundays, my three-hour diversion turned happily into nine. In January, 1992 Joe Gibbs led Washington to its third Super Bowl win.

It's been thirty-two years since Miriam died and I'm still a fan. It hasn't been easy. They've had new ownership and a revolving door of head coaches. Each April, during the draft, Larry and I hope the team's picks will bring more victories than defeats. A stronger offensive line? A more skilled quarterback? Last season, 2020, they actually, improbably, won their division and made it to the playoffs. Even though we're now living in Hawaii, I'll continue to watch them rebuild. And whether they even make it to the playoffs this year or not, let me just say this. Thanks, guys. Thanks for the great escape.

Half-time Notes

The NFL has installed new rules to address the huge risk and consequences of concussions. But I notice something. After each spectacular play, the players "atta boy" their teammate by tapping him on the helmet or even going gently helmet to helmet. It looks to me like, do enough of those, and they're giving each other mini-concussions. (Larry reminded me that the old "atta boy" was to give the player a congratulatory potch on his backside. Apparently, that's politically, socially, whatever ly incorrect today.)

Then there's the business of interviews. There should be a new NFL rule: No interviewing while the game is in progress. It interferes with our seeing the field. We miss plays! Even if the interview is in a box to the right of the field, we still miss the action; it's too small.

The interview questions—whether before, during, or after a game—are often inane. And predictably, so are the responses. The poor guys! A typical interviewer questioning the head coach (I'm only exaggerating a little): "It's halftime and your team is already three touchdowns behind. What are you going to do about it?" Or interviewing a quarterback after the game: "You threw the last-second interception that gave your opponents the Super Bowl win. How are you feeling?" It reminds me of Woody Allen's movie *Bananas*. The Latino rebel is lying on the church steps, dying. Woody, with microphone in the guy's face, asks him, "Are you upset?"

I Married My Bedroom Set

I wrote the following essay when we lived in Severna Park in our five-bedroom house with its spacious master bedroom. Today, in our quite crowded Honolulu condo, we still enjoy our bedroom set, but not quite so grandly.

If you come to my house to visit, you might have a hard time finding me. Because I plan to take up residence in our master bedroom with its new furniture. You'll find me kneeling at the shrine of my triple dresser. I'll be smiling at myself in my tri-fold mirror, press a discreet button, and behold! Discover the hidden green velvet panel studded with gold pegs. There I'll assemble my funky necklaces of wooden birds and glass beads.

This assemblage is not just a headboard, two dressers, a bachelor chest, mirror, and nightstand. Oh, no. This is wooden-ware worship, described in the manufacturer's brochure. "Romantic European bedroom collection influenced by the Empire era and King Louis Philippe. Pecan solids finished in a hand-rubbed golden fruitwood illuminating the natural wood grain."

In Judaism, when a bride and groom marry, they pledge their eternal fidelity to one another by signing a *ketubah*, a marriage contract. We are considering composing a furniture *ketubah*. It will read like this:

"Be sanctified unto us as our bedroom set. We will love, honor, and respect you, allowing no nicks or water marks to deface you. We promise to grace you with furniture polish and sustain you in your perfection. May there be peace in our bedroom and the confidence and serenity that come with knowing in our hearts that we have chosen wisely and within our budget."

Our arrival at this blissful state was not a straight and narrow path. Month after month, in each store, Larry and I asked ourselves: How can there be so much and we still can't find what we want? We entered a world of bedroom set styles that we hadn't know existed. Massive Greek Doric columns; but we didn't want to slumber in the Parthenon. Gracefully curved sleigh beds, where all we needed was the horse to pull us through the woods to Grandmother's house. Rough-hewn farmhouse beds for the penitent. Canopies draped with organdy, guaranteed to collect sky-borne dust bunnies. White lacquer, the Florida motel look.

We learned a new vocabulary, like "finials," ornaments that sit atop the tall bed posts. The finials look like swirls of soft ice cream before you take the first lick.

It was nobody's fault, of course, that our taste bore no resemblance to anything on the market. Running out of options, we finally headed to a huge discount store in Fredericksburg, Virginia. Last Chance Furniture Gulch, we called it. As we entered the store, I mumbled to Larry, "This better be good." And it was! We reached a decision and made a commitment to a masterpiece of pecan and marble.

My dedication to our boudoir was not quite complete. I was thinking of adding a codicil to my will. You see, I want to be buried with our headboard. There's plenty of room for Larry, too, if he so wishes. It's a queen-sized bed.

My headboard, my headstone. In the soft, rolling grasses of the cemetery will stand the pecan headboard with its elegant carved leaves. It will require an expanse of sixty-six inches, and the posts with their ice cream finials (yes, we bought those) will rise majestically into the sky, like arms reaching into the clouds.

What an appropriate resting place for a woman who loves to read in bed.

Chapter 9
MY JUDAISM

"Let us honor the generations that came before us, keeping the promise for those yet to be."

—*Mishkan T'Filah*, our Reform prayerbook

Growing Up Jewish - 145

Growing Up Jewish

My daughter, Miriam, came home from high school one day quite agitated. "You gave me a sandwich with bread for lunch! It's Passover week. We're only supposed to eat matzoh!" In the cafeteria the Jewish kids had chastised her. I was baffled. "Really?" At the Reform temple where I grew up in Milwaukee they never said a word.

My Reform temple had no *bar* or *bat mitzvahs*. No Hebrew classes. No fasting on *Yom Kippur*. We did have Sunday School, then Confirmation Class at age fifteen, and finally, Junior Congregation until we went off to college. I graduated from high school in 1953. I do not recall a single mention of the Holocaust at any time in my Jewish education. I do remember our rabbi telling us about Israeli independence; why the Jews chose Israel and not Uganda as the setting for the Jewish State.

My family only went to services on the High Holy Days. In the fall of 1957, we attended the morning *Yom Kippur* service, six months after my mother died. I was twenty-one. I sobbed throughout the entire service.

My father, son of Orthodox Jewish parents, was the youngest of five boys. His *Shabbat* chore, starting at age five, was to polish the sterling-silver candlesticks. Despite his dislike of organized religion, when Miriam, his first grandchild, died, he consulted our temple's rabbi. I was surprised, but deeply touched that he did. Was it for answers? There aren't any satisfying ones. There are evil people in the world and that's that.

When my ex-husband and I joined Temple Beth Shalom in Arnold, Maryland, I felt like an outsider. This Reform synagogue was quite traditional, with lots of Hebrew in the prayerbook and I didn't know any. I couldn't even follow the transliterations. A couple years later, Rabbi Robert Klensin offered a Beginning Prayerbook Hebrew class in his family room. Nine classes, two hours, once a week at night. The Klensins lived across the street, or I probably wouldn't have been motivated to go. But I did. There were eight of us women. We had a paperback textbook of seventy-eight pages: *Shalom Aleichem* (which means "Peace be to you") by Noah Golinkin, who says:

"Learn to Read the Hebrew Prayerbook! A textbook devoted specifically to teaching the skill of Hebrew reading to lay people in an adult education program....Now everyone can become part of our ancient heritage of praying in Hebrew."

I practiced each week out loud and did fairly well with the pronunciation. One session the rabbi couldn't be there, so the class was held at my house. A substitute Hebrew teacher came to lead us. She insisted that we get the pronunciation right. Well, one of our classmates (a friend, we all became friends in a way) just couldn't do it. She could not get the pronunciation right. She struggled, but perhaps she had a tin ear. The problem was, the teacher wouldn't let her off the hook. She kept correcting her without success. Meanwhile, the seven of us started laughing at the absurdity of it, not at our hapless friend, but at the teacher's refusal to let go, like a guarddog's teeth sunk in, clamped down, refusing to relinquish. Within seconds the rest of us were in stitches, unable to contain ourselves, gasping with laughter and tears. Finally, the teacher gave up and let our friend be with her stumbling pronunciation.

I had a weekly beauty parlor appointment for shampoo and set. My hairdresser was Gary Caplan, who did my hair for twenty years at the Golden Touch Salon in Severna Park. Gary grew up in an Orthodox Jewish home in Baltimore, where his parents owned a grocery store. During my nine weeks of prayerbook Hebrew classes, I would bring my slim text to my hair appointments and study it for half an hour while I sat under the dryer. If I showed up without my textbook, Gary shook his finger at me. "Where's your book?" I loved that he cared so much. After Miriam died, he said *Kaddish* for her every day for a year.

In case you might think that I became an accomplished reader of prayerbook Hebrew, I must tell you the truth. I actually have no facility for languages. To this day I can follow the Hebrew fairly well when the rabbi is reading, depending on how fast, but if I have to read it out loud myself, or even sing a fast song, I'm just as slow and clumsy as the substitute teacher's confused pupil. Somehow my brain never digested the finer points: two different "m's" depending on whether it's at the end of a word or not; two different "h's"; two different "f's." And on and on. That's why I'm in awe of the *bar* and *bat mitzvah* students. With ease they read from the Torah scrolls, which contain no vowels! Without vowels I'm sunk. Still, the transliterations in the prayerbook help a lot.

Doing my meager best with the Hebrew has great benefit for me. I feel that I'm part of the worldwide Jewish community. Accounting for differences in time zones, on *Shabbat* we are all reciting and singing the same prayers and songs in Hebrew, our ancient universal language.

Early in our marriage Larry and I were members of three synagogues. Mine: Temple Beth Shalom; Larry's: Congregation Kneseth Israel in Annapolis—"accommodating" Orthodox (using a Conservative prayerbook); and in 1993, when we retired and started wintering in Honolulu: Temple Emanu-El, where we now are, of course, full-time.

At our Friday night *Shabbat* service at Temple Emanu-El, Rabbi Ken Aronowitz has established a beautiful tradition. The small table holding the *Shabbat* candles sits on the floor in front of the bimah, on the same level as the seats. He invites *all* the women in attendance to come up and join in the singing of the Hebrew blessing. Sometimes there are as many as twenty of us, often including little girls, and even babies in their mothers' arms. I have never seen this tradition in any synagogue elsewhere. It makes us feel that we are all joined together, all connected.

There's an English translation that follows the Hebrew candle blessing. We didn't say it aloud; it appeared in our *siddur Mishkan T'Filah* and in the *Union Prayer Book* I grew up with. About two years ago, I got an inspiration that I felt would make it worth reciting aloud after the Hebrew. While we were still winter snowbirds, we began attending the Tuesday morning Jewish Wisdom class in the temple library, led at the time by Rabbi Morris

Goldfarb, of blessed memory. He was Rabbi Emeritus and resident scholar at Temple Emanu-El for thirteen years. During his class he created a phrase particularly joyful and uplifting: "Praised be Thou, Eternal God, Ever-present in our lives." I asked Rabbi Ken if I would be allowed to recite the blessing in English, opening with these words, after the Hebrew. He said yes. So it became my frequent Friday night tradition. I find it exhilarating that Rabbi Goldfarb is still participating in our service.

"Praised be thou, Eternal God, Ever-present in our lives, who has sanctified us by Thy commandments and commanded us to kindle the lights of Shabbat. May the lights bring you Sabbath peace. May the lights bring you Sabbath joy. Amen."

During COVID all our services are conducted via streaming.

Rabbi Ken has another tradition I have never seen elsewhere. During the multiple times we're required to stand, he says, "All rise, all rising in spirit." Thus, everyone present, even those who need to remain seated, feel that they too are participants.

We still attend the Tuesday morning Jewish Wisdom class (zooming now during COVID). At one session Sukkot had just ended. Maybe because Sukkot celebrates the harvest, the festival triggers a question I've always wanted answered. It's a Torah passage I find disturbing. In Genesis, chapter 4, Cain and Abel present their offerings to God. Abel, the shepherd, brings the choicest of his flock. Cain, the farmer, brings the fruit of the soil. God blesses Abel's offering, but ignores Cain's. Seeing Cain's disappointment, God asks him: "Why are you distressed, And why is your face fallen? Surely, if you do right, there is uplift, But if you do not do right sin crouches at the door."

This makes no sense to me. God does not provide a rational answer. I asked our rabbi why God rejects Cain's offering. Rabbi Ken smiles wisely and shrugs his shoulders. There is no answer.

Which brings me to reflect on other Torah stories that I have always found disturbing. Abraham agreeing to sacrifice Isaac; God putting Abraham in an impossible position. Rebecca favoring her son Jacob by brewing a plot to deprive Esau of his father's blessing. Laban forcing Jacob to work seven years before allowing him to marry Rachel. Then tricking him on his wedding night by forcing him to marry Leah instead, and making him work another seven years to finally marry Rachel. God not allowing Moses into the Promised Land.

The rabbis were the original writers of the Torah over a span of about 200 years. I've decided they were actually wannabe novelists centuries before novels were invented. They inserted conflict and suspense into the Torah's episodes and stories, including the whole range of human behavior, so that the Israelites would eagerly listen and want to hear more and more, to know how the stories ended. After all, literacy was unknown among the masses. It was all oral.

I think that's why the writers also assigned capriciousness to God Himself. They gave God a startling range of emotions, which would make Him more easily understood by the masses. The most blatant example is the Great Flood. God was angered by the wickedness of humanity, so he wiped out all living beings (except for those rescued in Noah's Ark). But why destroy innocent animals? They weren't to blame. God then sent up a rainbow and made a promise not to do that again. And on and on, where God exhibits dramatic swings of emotion.

The best answer I've ever heard to these difficult questions and painful predicaments was given to us by Rabbi Goldfarb. "In Reform Judaism we take the Torah seriously, but not literally."

At the beginning of my freshman year at Smith College, I found out we had a Hillel chapter, the international center for Jewish campus life. We had a rabbi. I went to a gathering and remember that very few of us attended; I recall nothing of substance about the meeting, except that I was introduced to the rabbi and told him I wanted to learn Yiddish. Oddly enough, he did not ask me how much Yiddish I knew. He barreled ahead and ordered me an expensive textbook, *College Yiddish*. If he had bothered to find out my level of knowledge he would have been shocked, because

I knew just three words: *chutzpah* (nerve); *zaftig* (plump, because I was); and *shmaltz* (chicken fat). I never even tried to study the book. Hillel at Smith didn't survive. I don't recall there ever being another meeting.

On an ordinary afternoon at Smith, one of the girls in my dorm changed the day to extraordinary. She was a junior named Florence Crown and she was walking down our fourth-floor hall with an astonishing announcement. "My uncle just bought the Empire State Building." She wasn't kidding. Her uncle was the Jewish philanthropist Henry Crown, an industrialist, who had started out life in America as an immigrant match-peddler's son.

I got divorced at age forty-five—after seventeen years of marriage, and faced the unpleasant process of dating again. My psychoanalyst father gave me a good idea when he called from Milwaukee for our Sunday noon chats. "Join some professional organizations," he said. I did. It sounded like a logical way to meet single people with my interests. I joined the Society of Professional Journalists (SPJ) and the National Press Club.

Before long, I met a journalist at SPJ named "Dennis." He was twice-divorced (which made me skeptical), but well-educated and a reporter for the *Baltimore Sun,* which impressed me. He was about my height and bland-looking, with glasses and medium-brown hair, and he invited me to dinner at Phillips Seafood House overlooking Baltimore's Inner Harbor. I accepted. At the very least, I would have an excellent free dinner that I didn't have to cook.

At dinner, we made small talk and he learned that I grew up in Milwaukee. Somehow we got on the subject of religion. "I'm Jewish," I told him.

"Oh, really? They have a colony out there in Milwaukee?"

Suddenly, the salmon in my belly started turning rancid and my jaw tightened. I looked at this man in total disbelief. A reporter for a major newspaper? From that moment on, he was history. I couldn't wait for the evening to end, and I merely went through the motions of civility. There was no answer to his ignorant question. What did he mean, "a colony"? The way he said it, it didn't even sound like a group of people; he made it sound more like a colony of bacteria in a Petri dish.

My near-silence the rest of the evening was borne out of shock. How could I even begin to explain how offensive his remark was? My ex-husband and I had fought for years about all kinds of stuff. But at least he was Jewish. Whatever our differences were, thinking of Jews as alien beings wasn't one of them.

The next day, my father called for our Sunday chat. I told him about my date and his appalling remark.

"You're taking it too seriously," Father replied.

"What? How can you say that?" I shot back.

"You could have reasoned with him and explained why he offended you."

"No, I couldn't. I'd rather stay home on Saturday nights."

Later, I thought about my father's reaction and why he took Dennis's remark so calmly. He was accustomed to this very reaction. He had been treating patients in psychotherapy and psychoanalysis for over forty years—generations of Milwaukeeans. Many of these patients were industrial barons, their wives, and their children. They were WASPS, White Anglo-Saxon Protestants. They weren't anti-Semitic. It's just that many of them, before they came to my father, had never met a single Jew in their entire lives!

But I have never acquired my father's equanimity—his composure under stress, his ability to enlighten with humor, to teach without seeming to teach, undefensively, without preaching, without anger. He always gave people the benefit of the doubt and felt they were capable of understanding. And by the time they left him—emotionally stronger—they knew something about what a Jew was.

I'd had my own indelible experience with the WASP world of elegant Milwaukee. I wrote about it in my memoir *Love! Laugh! Panic! Life with My Mother* in my chapter "The Debutante," when I was the token Jew. I also talked proudly about my grandfather Harry Bragarnick. A Russian immigrant in 1913, he refused to change his name at Ellis Island. In an era when Jews weren't so accepted in the advertising world, Grandpa's son also kept his name. My uncle Robert Bragarnick was a Madison Avenue executive and a founder of the magazine *Food and Wine.*

Sometimes God speaks to me in mysterious ways. Once I put money in a snack machine and pressed the button for my choice. The vending machine ate my dollar. No Milky Way came out. I figured God was sending chocoholic me a message: "Do not eat candy bars!"

And on August 14, 2020, Larry was due for surgery at Pali Momi Hospital at 6:45 a.m. We needed to be up by 4:30 a.m. I awoke on the dot of 4:30—but not because the alarm rang. It did not go off. I had set it wrong, accidentally for 4:30 in the afternoon. I fervently thanked God for getting me up on time.

On January 6th of this year, our country witnessed the terrifying assault on the U.S. Capitol by Trump supporters.

The inauguration of President Joe Biden was scheduled for Wednesday, January 20th.

On Friday night January 15th, Rabbi Ken streamed our *Shabbat* service, on the eve of the Martin Luther King, Jr. birthday weekend. The rabbi is always finely tuned to what is going on in the world, providing us with understanding, comfort, and guidance. On that Friday night, he sang our traditional *Shabbat* song "*Michamochah.*" The words are "Who is like you, O God...Your children witnessed your sovereignty, the sea splitting before Moses and Miriam..." He sang it in Hebrew, but to the tune of "We Shall Overcome," Martin Luther King, Jr.'s signature song of hope. Then he sang "We Shall Overcome" in English. He ended with a prayer for a peaceful inauguration and followed it by singing "God Bless America."

Participating in the service at home, we sang along with him.

Chapter 10
MEDICAL MISHAPS

"Isn't it a bit unnerving that doctors call what they do 'practice'?" —**George Carlin**

Grieving over My Stupidity

December 14, 2019. We had just arrived at a holiday party in an elegant Honolulu home. We'd been to this house before. I knew that the spacious living room had a single six-inch step leading down into the dining room. I reminded Larry of it. He wandered into the kitchen while I stopped in the bathroom. Ten minutes later, I was standing in the living room. A woman I didn't know was coming toward me. She was at least ten feet away. Illogically, I backed up.

Off the step. And fell backward onto the marble floor of the dining room. I could feel myself falling, slamming down with a massive thud on my right hip and back. Unable to move. But I was in denial. "No ambulance," I told a solicitous guest, Susan, who was gently, wisely, kneeling with me. We talked. Or I tried to.

Guests had been told to bring an unwrapped gift for a needy child. I loved what I had bought, and I tried to describe it to Susan. She was listening, but I could hear my voice floundering, my speech garbled. I was unable to describe it! An alarm bell went off in my mind. Was I having a stroke?

Susan asked me again. "An ambulance?" This time I murmured yes. The EMTs arrived almost immediately and off we went to the ER at Queens Medical Center. Lying there, with the EMT sitting behind my head, I began talking to him. Now my brain had cleared and I talked at length. I'm not sure about what. But it wasn't scrambled.

In the ER, the CT scan showed two closed-compression fractures in the lumbar region of my spine, meaning the lower back.

Eek! I broke my back! I asked the ER doctor how long it would take me to heal.

"Several months," he said.

Yikes!

Grieving over My Stupidity Again

I should not have to write this, but perhaps writing it will issue me a more tangible warning than if I just re-hash it in my head. You've heard of the book *Smart Women, Foolish Choices?* It's mainly about choosing the wrong man as your spouse. For now, it's not a matter of foolish choices, but of no-brainer behavior.

January, 2020. It was now five weeks after my fall at the party. I was wearing a Depend at night, something I never dreamed I'd ever have to. At 2:00 a.m. I should have made a potty stop but I didn't; too tired. I fell back asleep. At 6:00 a.m. I woke up realizing I needed the bathroom instantly! But because I was still recovering from my fall with residual left-hip soreness, I needed to get out of bed very very slowly. But instead of just letting the Depend do its job, I struggled to get up and to the bathroom anyway. I only got a few feet. In front of my dresser I tripped and fell—flat on my face. Blood gushed from my nose, all over the rug and me.

Larry woke up, started mopping me up, and we talked about whether we should go to Islands Urgent Care, just a mile or two away. I dragged myself to my computer and Googled it—with my left hand pressing a towel to my nose. They were closed, for Martin Luther King, Jr. Day. Besides, I was in no position to drive. Then I suggested we call the paramedics (who are at the fire station right around the corner). "No," Larry said, "call Jackie, It looks like you're going to need stitches." I did. I had a cut and stripe of blood going about three inches down from the bridge of my nose. Jackie got to our place in twenty minutes and drove me straight to the Queens ER. We were there 5-½ hours. Finally, Jackie was allowed to bring me home, then went to Sam's Club for my prescribed antibiotic.

I sat down at the kitchen table and sobbed, noisily, to get lots of Larry's sympathetic attention.

"Don't cry," he begged.

"I want to!" I wailed—in frustration and shame, and because I had a nice morning mapped out for myself. To go to Don Quijote, leisurely, using the grocery cart as a walker. My treat for the day. Now, no way. Later, Jackie and Rodney went for us. Although they were too kind to say so, I ruined their Martin Luther King holiday together.

I was now gorgeously decorated with purple bruises around my right eye and down both cheeks. Stunning. Purple's my favorite color.

Before Jackie and Rodney left us at ten o'clock at night, Jackie gave me a final bit of advice. It was about time I learned it. "Sit down and think about what you're doing before you do it!"

Meet Wally the Wheelchair

In 2006 Larry had a minor heart attack. At least that's what the cardiologist in Annapolis called it. Nevertheless, for us a "minor" heart attack was anything but. It was an unwelcome permanent guest, the gorilla in the living room, lurking in a virtual La-Z-Boy recliner.

Still, Larry recovered quickly, and I assumed we had successfully climbed the Mount Everest of physical nightmares. Don't ask me why I assumed it, what with our ages of seventy-five and seventy-eight. Little did I know, we were about to wrestle with a case of Back to the Future.

Larry's back, that is. He went through a litany of cures, including surgery. Home free, right? Wrong. Five years later, he lapsed back to square one. He could only walk about a hundred yards—with two canes. With his wry sense of humor, he dubbed them Cane and Able, a variation of the biblical spellings. But they could only help part-time. So my retired engineer husband came up with an idea: a transportable wheelchair, the kind that gets pushed.

We took a chance and bought it online. Made of shiny black steel, it had little wheels, and came with a soft gray cushion. It weighed only nineteen pounds, and was light enough, the manual said, to collapse and fit in our car trunk. Larry named it Wally.

And now the fun began. Wally had nice removable footrests,

which we slid into place. Larry sat down—and immediately announced, "Forget this!" He has long legs. When he placed his feet on the footrests, his knees came up nearly to his chin. He removed his feet, yanked the footrests off, and tossed them aside. So what to do now? Pedal with his feet? Of course not. There was only one choice: for him to hold up his large, heavy legs while I pushed. Already not ideal; how could he keep them up for more than a few yards without tiring?

* * * *

I had never been in the position of conspicuous caregiver, out in public, one for all the world to see. Always before, Larry's complicated health "issues" were hidden to the naked eye. (I love this current word "issues." A physical or emotional dysfunction, even a huge one, is now an "issue.")

Well, I thought, *now's my chance to excel at an entirely new skill. I'll become the Olympic gold medal wheelchair pusher.* From our house in Severna Park, we drove to the B&A Trail. It was only a few minutes from home. Before Larry's back issue, we easily walked two miles on the trail twice a week.

So here we were, out for Wheelchair Wally's maiden voyage. *Push. Grunt. Push. Grunt.* After five minutes, my arms were already aching. *How come?* I wondered. Then I reverted to scolding myself. *Get a grip! You're not exactly a weak person. You've been going to Jazzercise for thirty years, lifting eight-pound hand weights.*

But this was different. The trail looked flat, but it actually had imperceptible rises, surprising me as I was pushing. Also, the asphalt pavement was not entirely smooth.

Now I was panting. I could feel my heart working out double-time. "This is not easy," I whined.

Push some more. We conversed. Or tried to. Larry talked to me, but because he was facing straight ahead and I was behind Wally, I couldn't hear him. "Dear, what did you say? You're talking to the air. You have to turn your head toward me."

"What? And get a crick in my neck?"

Push some more. My quads and calves were tightening up.

157

Hey, maybe that's a good thing, I tried to convince myself. Seven minutes later I stopped. "This is too hard!" I wailed.

"What's so hard?" Larry asked, a reprimand in his tone. "You're not doing the work. It's the wheels doing it."

Now I was steamed. "You think? I'm pushing 230 pounds!"

"Huh? No you're not."

"Oh yes I am," I retorted. "You weigh 210, plus the wheelchair and cushion weigh twenty."

"Oh."

So much for our trail outings.

Next we tried the mall. *This should be easy,* I thought. *Smooth, wide, tiled corridors.* Larry settled into Wally. I was hoping we'd bump into friends—I was feeling quite experienced tooling him along. Until we entered Macy's. The floors in the main aisles were smooth, but in the Men's Department, browsing among the actual clothes, I encountered carpeting. Not so easy. Still, I blithely wheeled Wally around the clothes racks like a slalom skier, when I heard, "Hey, cut it out!" Only then did I realize that he was getting slapped in the face by shirts, pants, and jackets.

The escalator was out of the question, of course, so we introduced Wally to its maiden voyage in the elevator. The shoppers inside thoughtfully stepped to the left and right walls, creating a clear shot for us through the center. I was thinking, *Look at me, everyone! Good caregiver!* For our excursion to the mall I had insisted that Larry use the footrests. Briskly, I pushed Wally inside the elevator. *Slam!* We hit the back wall.

"Ow!" Larry muttered. It hadn't occurred to me that the footrests protrude out, with his size twelve feet extending even farther forward. This was a lesson I never mastered.

As we were leaving the store, a young saleswoman offered to hold one of Macy's heavy glass doors open for us. I repaid her kindness by rolling Wally onto her sandal. Nimbly, she managed to slide her bare foot away, but her sandal toe was still stuck under Wally's right front wheel. I apologized profusely. Out in the main corridor, I caught my breath and stifled my near-panic. I had narrowly escaped the prospect of visiting the poor woman in the hospital—with her broken toe that I had caused, plus paying her medical bills.

Back in our minivan, we both simmered with frustration. I broke the silence. "You're too grouchy. You criticize my every move when I'm pushing you. I can't do anything right." At a red light, I apologized for being hypersensitive and defensive.

"I'm sorry, too," he said. "I hate the feeling of being dependent. At least when I drive a car I have control. When I'm in Wally, it's like whirling through space without a steering wheel."

I truly did understand. He's a strong, resourceful man, extremely motivated and determined to get well, and it hurt me to see him like this.

For several years I tried lifting Wally into the car without my husband's help—but always hoping bystanders were watching. Showing off! Proud of my strength even at age eighty-one. And then one morning, a few years later, I couldn't get out of bed. My back wouldn't let me. Pride goeth before the doctor and a CT scan. I had destroyed three discs lifting too-heavy things. The price of showing off! After a month of physical therapy, I was cured. So, when would I be free to lift heavy things again and prove that my new age of eighty-four had nothing on me? Never.

* * * *

Larry's obstinate back refused to improve on its own. We faced the prospect of a second surgery and consulted a spine surgeon—recommended by Larry's pain management physician. The surgeon explained the risks. "You could emerge from it no better, or even worse off than before. During surgery you could suffer a heart attack or stroke. You could die. Even with a favorable outcome, recovery could take a year, maybe even longer."

Wonderful. I threw my escape mechanism into gear, shifting my thoughts to our kitchen cabinet where I hid my consolation snack: tiny Oreos dipped in fudge. I would dive in the minute we got home. No sharing with my husband, thank you. He was overweight and I wasn't!

In June, 2010, Larry endured ten hours of surgery to reconstruct his spine. He pulled through it so well that within a few days he was transferred to a rehab hospital. I assumed he'd be there a week or two, at least. The very next day, Larry announced to me: "I'm going home!"

"No!" I shouted. "You just got here." He glared at me, fire in his eyes, and if looks could kill, yes, I'd be dead. But I was envisioning myself as helpless caregiver, unable to lift him, turn him, or anything else. On the other hand, the nurses weren't so thrilled with their new patient. Was he an Evel Knievel copycat? Larry was zooming around in his heavy-duty hospital wheelchair, entertaining himself by doing wheelies down the hall and around corners.

For the next two days the staff put him through his paces. He wasn't allowed to go home until he could accomplish a long list of daily tasks, like climbing stairs, dressing himself, and standing for five minutes at the kitchen counter. "We want you to be able to make yourself a sandwich." He aced everything.

But when I arrived to visit on Thursday morning, Larry's face was contorted in anger. "I'm going home and you can't stop me!" The night before, something bad happened.

Late in the evening, a nurse's aide marched into the room and announced to Larry: "I'm here to put in your catheter."

"What?" he roared. "I'm not getting a catheter."

"Oh yes you are," she said.

"You take one more step and I'll throw this pitcher of ice water at you."

She kept coming.

Larry boomed, "You come one step closer and I'll throw this full bottle of urine at you!"

An RN, a registered nurse, burst into the room, shouting. "No, no, not him! It's for the other man!"

Larry's roommate, a stroke victim, was laughing till the tears came. *He* had ordered the catheter.

Thursday, June 18th, the rehab hospital agreed to let Larry come home, after only four days. He had passed all his occupational and physical therapy tests.

Recovery went well. To celebrate, we arranged to meet friends at our favorite diner on Halloween night. We left Wally in the car trunk and entered the restaurant. Larry plodded along with Cane and Able. Our friends were already seated across the room. Eager to join them, I strode ahead of him and accidentally kicked Cane on Larry's right side. In his resonant bass voice, he bellowed, "You almost knocked me over!"

"Oops! Sorry, dear." I spun around and tried again to move ahead of him, this time on his left side, but now I tripped over Able.

"Hey, stop it!" Larry thundered. Fifty diners—or was it a hundred?—laid down their forks and turned toward us. They were probably all thinking, *Oh, that poor man with the two canes and his wretched, incompetent caregiver.*

Happy Halloween.

Ten years later Larry still has two canes, but rarely uses them. He now has a three-wheeled "rollator" walker to maneuver in our little apartment. He calls it Rollie. He's still plagued with chronic pain, which he suffers in silence.

And where's Wally? He resides in a corner of our living room, collapsed, lonesome and despondent, suffering from low self-esteem. Larry uses him only if we attend all-day meetings or book signings (which are nonexistent during COVID-19)—or to navigate the long halls in the office buildings for doctors' appointments. Or relaxing at Magic Island, where he sits comfortably in Wally reading a book, while I'm taking a short hike of my own.

Now if only his pain would take a hike.

The Tooth About Me

I have lousy teeth. I didn't realize how lousy until I finished college and moved to Boston for my first real job. Thus began a string of firsts.

My first toothache as a Smith College graduate sent me to a Harvard Dental School faculty member. With great skill and at huge expense (sticking my father with the bill, of course), he installed four permanent bridges. But at my first appointment, before the dentist even entered the room, his dutiful technician loomed over me. Like a serpent ready to strike, she hissed: "You don't just have multiple cavities. You need to floss. Your gums are a mess!"

They were? You could've fooled me. I thought everyone routinely got painful toothaches. My educated professional parents had teeth that looked nice but behaved miserably. Not their fault. They were born in 1904 and 1908, the children of Russian immigrants. Who knew about dental hygiene back then? Mother had a couple of removable bridges, and from the way she often took them out and tried to reposition them, I could tell they were mighty uncomfortable. Our family dentist, whom I'll call Dr. Clueless, must have snoozed off during his Dental Hygiene classes. We never once heard him utter the word "floss."

I assume he knew about it. According to the website Tooth-brushExpress.com, floss is an age-old invention. "Researchers have found dental floss and toothpick grooves in the teeth of prehistoric humans....A New Orleans dentist promoted flossing with a piece of silk thread in 1815."

For fifty years I conveniently blamed my bad teeth on the neglectful Dr. Clueless and my parents' dental DNA, which I'd unfortunately inherited.

But a few months ago, I realized that I am largely, very largely, responsible for my fate. The descent into dental hell began my senior year at Smith, when a classmate and I spent significant hours in a coffee shop on Green Street—bordering the Smith campus in Northampton, Massachusetts. Our ritual: coffee, cigarettes, and finally, peppermint breath mints to kill the tobacco taste and odor. Let's not even talk about the evils of smoking. In 1957, who knew? To me it was just a mark of sophistication. I never ran across a single article saying "Quitting Smoking Can Save Your Teeth." I finally did quit at the age of twenty-four. By then, the cigarettes had already caused plenty of damage.

For years and years, I popped breath mints and hard candies. Only a few calories apiece, I always assured myself.

When I moved to New York for a better job, my new dentist asked me: "Are you a cake and candy eater?" I refused to respond, but he already knew the answer from a swift glance at my hips. "Rinse afterward," he ordered. I didn't. I couldn't be bothered.

I've discovered a downside to the wonderful permanent bridges. They look and act like real teeth, but they're not as sharp. In restaurants, this means everyone else at the table is done, their plates have been cleared, and I'm still chewing. Half my meal gets relegated to a box for home.

During the four decades I lived in Maryland I endured endless fillings, root canals, implants, new permanent bridges, the works. At one appointment I confessed to my dental hygienist, "I keep butterscotch hard candies in my purse. They're delicious and only a few calories."

"What?" she shrieked. "I'd rather you ate ten chocolate bars than one piece of hard candy!"

"I also suck on cough drops," I whispered, cowering in the chair.

She nearly fell off her vinyl-padded stool. "Those are even worse! They're designed to coat the throat, so they coat the teeth as well and cause decay." Her drill-sergeant instruction: "Go sugar-free!"

I did. But going sugarless was just the beginning. Now my mornings begin with a labor-intensive five-step routine. Nothing can supercede it. Not even if the fire alarm in our building goes off.

- Rinse with water within twenty minutes of eating; you can cut your cavity rate by thirty percent. This unsightly activity takes place at the kitchen sink. My kind husband pretends not to notice.

- Brush.
- . Floss.
- Use Water-Pik. But only before dressing, unless I want water trickling up my sleeve and splashing on my silk blouse.
- Rinse for one minute with the fluoride mouthwash ACT.

Do not eat or drink anything for thirty minutes afterward.

And that's just my after-breakfast ritual. Or should I call it penance?

It seems to be working. I just had a perfect checkup. Alas, however, my Honolulu dentist felt compelled to deliver a solemn pronouncement.

"If only you'd started all this years ago."

A Bridge to Nowhere

June, 2010. I was going to the MVA to renew my driver's license. I waited my forty-five minutes, took my eye test, and it was time for my picture. I flashed a broad smile. The clerk handed me my new license and away I went. I got in the car and took it out of my wallet to really study it, for the first time. There I was with my huge, happy smile—missing my three almost-front teeth. I'd forgotten to put in my temporary removable bridge before I left the house. Oh, well, it wouldn't be long before I could renew my license again and get a new picture taken. Only five years.

Once I forgot my temporary bridge on a Friday night when we were on our way to Temple Emanu-El for *Shabbat* services. We were almost there in heavy rush-hour traffic. It was definitely too late to go back home to retrieve my bridge. Have you ever tried to smile without opening your lips? People think you're smirking at them.

I was lying flat on my back in the dental chair, wishing I were anywhere else but there. I was getting all numbed before the oral surgeon came back in to begin yet another implant procedure. His technician, who looked like she was still in grade school, leaned over me and said, "So how's your day going?"

Buying a Mouthwash? Hah!

Thirty years ago, buying ACT mouthwash was a simple matter. But today it's a different story. The manufacturer won't leave us consumers alone with one easy decision: ACT Mouthwash. At the supermarket I'm confronted with a bewildering array. This is just one example of manufacturers blitzing us with too many choices.

So, back home, I went to the ACT website to find out which one might be best for me, and here's what I discovered was being offered for adults.

1. ACT Total Care Anticavity
2. ACT Restoring Mouthwash Mint Burst
3. ACT Restoring Anticavity
4. ACT Mint Anticavity Fluoride
5. ACT Mint Fluoride Rinse
6. ACT Dry Mouth Anticavity Fluoride Mouthwash
7. ACT Cool Mint Restoring Fluoride Rinse
8. ACT Advanced Care Plaque Guard
9. ACT Anticavity Iced Sweet Mint

And that's not even taking into account the ones for children: ACT Kids Variety Mouthwash Pack—four different bottles, including Bubblegum Blowout.

I can't help but wonder: Are they all the same product given different names by the company's marketing department?

Which brings to mind a quote written by the philosopher William Dean Howells a hundred years ago, but still relevant here. "See how today's achievement is only tomorrow's confusion."

Chapter 11
ON WRITING TOGETHER

"Writing is the most powerful idea we humans have ever come up with."—"The First Alphabet" on *NOVA*

The Good, the Bad, and the Cozy

When you're a husband and wife writing team, how do you create a novel or story that comes out seamless, sounding like one author?

In my chapter "Life with Larry" I said that he was going to write a novel and wanted me to help him. True to his word, when he retired he wrote the first draft of *Cry Ohana, Adventure and Suspense in Hawaii.* Then handed it to me, "Your turn." We were the halt leading the blind. Many drafts, titles, and years later, we published it; it's always been our most popular Hawaii book.

We write back-to-back on dueling computers in our little home office (really our second bedroom). So, in the beginning, how did we handle the writing process?

Larry: You cut that whole paragraph. I worked for hours on it.

Me: Less is more, darling.

Larry: Oh yeah? You gave the grocery bagger a backstory.

Me: You're squashing my creativity.

Larry: You're trimming my subordinate clauses.

Me: You're acting like a spoiled brat.

Larry: I can't stand to hear a woman cry.

Our jousting was usually short-lived. I'd sigh and submit. Larry would lick his wounds, and we'd resign ourselves to the compromises required. Maalox helped, too.

Here are excerpts of the article we did for *City Book Review* (San Francisco) and as a blog interview for *Book Cover Junkie.*

What is the best thing about a husband and wife writing team?

Larry: You're never writing in a vacuum. There's always someone close by to listen to your story's direction and your choice of words. The helping hand when you can't find that ever-so-right word or story twist is a godsend.

Me: We read our final drafts aloud to each other. The inconsistencies and awkward phrases really pop out at us.

What is the worst thing about a husband and wife writing team?

Larry: If you'll excuse my Latin, there's this *co-writus interruptus* thing. Working back-to-back in the same room, it's too easy to stop her and ask: "Does adrenaline have an e?" rather than look it up myself.

Me: I'm just as bad. Maybe worse. "Dear?" (No answer, so I barrel on anyway.) "Does a revolver have a safety?"

There are times when Larry gets a little wordy; cute but wordy. So I'll do what I call "judicious pruning," an expression I learned as an assistant editor at *Harper's Magazine*. Larry calls it "slash and burn." Then, with sleeves rolled up, we negotiate. In our early days, I would not have received a doctorate in diplomacy. I'm a little better now.

Larry's greatest strength as a writer is his imagination, his inventiveness. He says he's more devious than I am, so he conjures up all our plots and writes the first draft. Most days he's at the computer for five to six hours of writing. He has a much longer attention span than I have.

Larry: She *could* work a little faster. We're getting behinder by the day. Her strength as a writer? She has this wonderful feel for people and human nature. So she breathes life into my minimalist characters: physical appearance, sharpening the dialogue. Sometimes she adds a scene for more conflict. She'll take an anecdote I told second-hand and turn it into real-time drama, like an ugly shouting match in a restaurant.

Me: What can get in the way of our working together is my own nonfiction writing life: personal essays (including some award-winners) and my memoirs. *Love! Laugh! Panic! Life with My Mother* is the most recent. *Miriam's World—and Mine* is my second memoir of our beloved daughter Miriam Luby Wolfe.

[In my final chapter here, you'll have the opportunity to read all about Miriam.]

In terms of writing, what are you most likely to disagree on?

Larry: When Rosemary comes up with her mixed metaphors. And when she edits my stuff ruthlessly! She even tweaks my one-page business letters.

Me: Hah! Stephen King said, "To write is human. To edit is divine." Harlan Coben's take: "If somebody tells me he doesn't rewrite, I don't want to party with him."

Larry: Somehow we've managed to write ten novels and three books of short stories, with more to come, and haven't killed each other yet!

How are you most like your protagonists Dan and Rivka Sherman?

Larry: We made them like us, but much younger: a Jewish couple in their early fifties. Dan and Rivka abandon thriving careers as an editor and electronics engineer (which we were) to buy the fictional Olde Victorian Bookstore in Annapolis, Maryland.

Me: Physically, Dan is his own man. Tall and gangly, he sprawls when he sits. He has bushy black hair and eyebrows. The only thing that's thin about Larry is his gray hair. However, Dan's personality is very much like Larry's: analytical and practical, a born problem-solver. Rivka is a lot like me. Feisty—I came out of the womb arguing; affectionate; and addicted to chocolate. In *Death Goes Postal* she finds herself in a hopeless situation and prays. "Please, God, if you help me escape I'll never ask you for another thing. And I promise not to argue with Dan so much. I'll eat a piece of chocolate before opening my mouth. And I'll never again snitch blueberry muffins during *Yom Kippur* fast."

Why do you think bookstore owners make good sleuths?

Larry: They must be intellectuals and extroverts. But Dan and Rivka think they're buying into a pleasant, predictable life. Instead, they become reluctant sleuths in the wake of a mugging, robbery, kidnapping—and murder.

Me: Which makes them all the more fun.

We've used a sprinkling of our own experiences in our fiction. In *Hot Grudge Sunday,* sleuths Paco and Molly are on their honeymoon out West. Their itinerary is based on a tour we took, but we've installed hair-raising consequences at each site, ending at the Grand Canyon. In *Copper and Goldie,* Sam is disabled; he walks with two canes. Larry gave Sam his own chronic back trouble; he too walks with two canes. Sam's Auntie Momi asks him: "You still walkin' wit' dem giant chopsticks?"

My Quirky Crusade

A zillion books, articles, and workshops are out there on how to be a better writer. If you put them end to end they'd probably circle the earth.

In the writing of dialogue, there's a current style these days for authors of mystery and suspense fiction. The standard appears to be the verb "said." For instance, "I feel miserable," she said. "My car broke down," he said.

We're taught that "said" is a good verb and we should use it—and rarely anything else. And, above all, ditch the adverbs! Here are a few examples of adverbs that tell instead of show:

"…she said angrily, spitefully, sweetly, happily, morosely." Instead of showing: "I'll never come back," she shouted.

Elmore Leonard (author of *Get Shorty*) said something like "Let's kill all the adverbs." Lawrence Block wrote a book for writers: *Telling Lies for Fun and Profit.* He said that if your characters are good and your dialogue is natural, "let them talk to each other. And stay the hell out of their way."

The same rule goes for piling on the adjectives. The Maryland Writers' Association newsletter once had a cartoon of a speaker at a podium in front of a large audience. A sign on the wall behind him read: "Adjectives and Adverbs Anonymous."

But getting back to the word "said." I'm launching my own personal crusade to do away with the persistence of it. My point is, the word "said" is boring. Downright booooring! I miss the old-fashioned authors' extravagant animal sounds, such as: "He barked, he yelped, he bayed, he grunted." "She snarled, she screeched, she warbled, she bleated."

Now I ask you: Aren't those verbs more fun? I intend to indulge in them. But I promise you, I will never write "The horse-faced woman neighed" or "whinnied." You have my word on that.

Malice and Mayhem
In the Drip (not Grip) of a Dilemma

Annual conventions for mystery writers and fans proliferate throughout the U.S. They have hypnotic names like Killer Nashville, Crimebake, Left Coast Crime, Sleuthfest, Murder and Mayhem, and ThrillerFest. (During COVID they're being Zoomed. It's a painful but necessary compromise.)

For nearly twenty years Larry and I happily attended one of the larger ones, Malice Domestic. Celebrating the traditional mystery, Malice was inspired by Agatha Christie's detective novels. The cunning name comes from *Macbeth*. "Duncan is in his grave; after life's fitful fever he sleeps well; treason has done his worst; nor steel nor poison, malice domestic, foreign levy, nothing can touch him further."

We were attending Malice Domestic XIX at the Crystal Gateway Marriott in Arlington, Virginia. I had ducked out of the afternoon panels for an energetic few laps in the hotel pool. Big mistake. The Jacuzzi was as cold as an iced latte, and when I plunged into the pool, a surge of hot water rolled over me. I tried to explain this bizarre mix-up to the smiling pool attendant, but he couldn't speak a word of English. Or pretended not to. And now I was about to miss the interview with the wonderful Guest of Honor Rochelle Krich. I hastily toweled off, then slipped nylon shorts over my wet swimsuit.

I was standing at the second-floor elevator in a puddle of swimming pool water. The elevator doors opened. *Ah, space for one more.* I stepped in, the doors closed. *Oh, no, I miscalculated.* The elevator was so full I couldn't turn around to face forward.

Even worse, just behind the panel of floor buttons, stood a bride! Her white taffeta wedding gown flared out at the hips, a quarter-inch from my water-soaked shorts; her lace hem almost tickled my squeegee-ing flip-flops. The groom hovered anxiously behind her, elegant in his military dress uniform with gold braid looped at the shoulders. Were they en route to the ceremony? Or fleeing from the reception? I couldn't quite tell.

My brain lurched into overdrive. How many rules of elevator etiquette had I already broken? About fifty. *Fineliving.com's* first rule: "Face forward and don't stare." *Good Housekeeping.com's* rule number two: "If the car's crowded, ask someone to push the button for your floor." Should I have snapped a command to the bride? "Ten, please!"

With no way to escape, I murmured an apology in my best Miss Manners imitation: "Oh, dear, I should have waited for the next one." Whereupon I silently prayed that I wouldn't spray indelible chlorinated drops on the bride's shimmering gown.

But she shrugged prettily, waved her hand over her billowing skirt, and said, "This thing? It's already dirty." Grace under pressure, as Hemingway would say. Her groom beamed with joy.

Published in Not Everyone's Cup of Tea: *An Interesting and Entertaining History of Malice Domestic's First 25 Years. Wildside Press (2013). The anthology was a 2014 Agatha Award nominee.*

Envy

That very night (during the same Malice convention) Larry and I attended the awards banquet. During the few minutes between dinner and the speeches, I hurried to the ladies' room. I was standing in line behind a woman with blonde hair, a straight skirt that came to her knees, and fishnet stockings on long, slender legs. I studied them with envy. Impulsively, I turned to the short, chunky woman in line behind me. I didn't know her, but felt enough kinship to whisper, "In my next life maybe I'll get to wear those stockings." She giggled and said, "Me too."

Back at our table, the presentations began and I discovered that the lady with the legs was Laura Lippman, author of mystery and crime novels. I sighed. A best-selling novelist *and* perfect legs? How unfair is that?

The Case of the Missing Diamonds

Miguel de Cervantes, the immortal author of *Don Quixote*, once said, "My memory is so bad that many times I forget my own name." Hard to believe. But his confession did sparkle with recognition as I thought of my gorgeous diamond earrings, a birthday gift from Larry.

A couple years later, we were attending Malice Domestic, this time in Bethesda, Maryland, as well as participating on panels. Back in our hotel room after the Saturday night banquet, I casually looked in the mirror and shrieked: "My diamond earrings—they're gone! They must have fallen off my earlobes in the banquet room!" Still wearing my silk suit, I rushed to the elevator and back downstairs. On hands and knees, I frantically searched the rug under what had been our table. Nothing. I asked a waiter who was cleaning up. "No, ma'am," he said. "Haven't seen any earrings."

Suddenly, I found myself transformed into a person I didn't even recognize: mean-spirited, vicious, vengeful. Still crawling around under the table, I asked myself: *What if another author or mystery fan found them? What if she saw the earrings lying on the rug, watched us leave the banquet room, then casually dropped her purse*

173

next to the table. And in the guise of picking it up, scooped up my ear-rings and adopted them for herself?

A slight gust whipped around me as the waiter removed the tablecloth. Bending low, he glared down at me, puzzled, suspicious, and I was jolted into reality. If an attendee had swiped them, I would have to stalk 800 guests trying to find her. And then what? *Crazy me*, I decided, as I dragged myself back up to our room.

For two years I mourned the loss of my earrings. One day, rummaging in a file cabinet in our home office, I saw a tiny green box under a folder. I popped it open. My diamond earrings! Stowed where no burglar could ever find them. I had never taken them to Malice in the first place!

Left Coast Crime

In addition to Malice Domestic, we attended many Left Coast Crime mystery conventions. Here are some authoritative comments I learned at LCC in Phoenix, Arizona, in 2016.

- You can't actually suffocate someone in the trunk of a car.
- You only need to recite the Miranda rights if you have arrested someone and plan to interrogate him or her in custody.
- Joseph Waumbaugh, author of *The New Centurions* and *The Blue Knight*: "What's interesting is not how cops work on cases, but how cases work on cops."
- Canadians do not carry guns. They have far fewer mass shootings in Canada than we do. Cops in the U.S. have much greater stress because of the prevalence of guns.

The 2017 Left Coast Crime convention was a milestone for us. Our Sisters in Crime/Hawaii Chapter hosted "Honolulu Havoc" at the Hilton Hawaiian Village. Larry and I were the panel co-chairs. We spent a year working to fit 160 authors into the most effective slots—often amid cancellations due to blizzards, health issues, or even financial setbacks. But it was an exhilarating four days, kicking off with the sunset over Waikiki, and ending with feedback from one author: "Best convention I ever attended."

Getting Personal
To Enhance Our Fiction

Larry and I use both first-hand research and personal experiences to enhance our novels and stories.

One of our newest books is *Copper and Goldie, 13 Tails of Mystery and Suspense in Hawaii.* Sam Nahoe, a disabled ex-cop-turned-cabbie, and his golden retriever (with a touch of Doberman), take on Honolulu bank robbers, kidnappers, and vengeful wives. Even killers, compelling Sam to get his P.I. license. In "The Snake Lady" Sam's Auntie Momi visits her fortune teller, but finds her dead—murdered—and Heki, her gentle pet python, missing.

But wait! Snakes are illegal in the Aloha State. Detective Danny groans. "Not another damn reptile. No matter how hard we try, the black market thrives." We researched how Hawaii deals with these illegal critters. The penalty is up to three years in prison and a $200,000 fine. But the Department of Agriculture has an amnesty plan: Turn it in, no questions asked, no penalties.

Our research was satisfying, but our plot was at a standstill. It was missing an irrefutable piece of evidence that would nail the killer. A happy personal coincidence solved our problem—and the case. Our cousin Susan Saul, a master jewelry designer in Atlanta, had just posted her newest creation on Facebook: an exotic snake ring! With her delighted permission, we incorporated the ring into our plot.

Near the conclusion, the story reads this way: "As Valerie angrily crossed her bare arms over her chest, Sam's gaze landed on her left hand. Exposed on her third finger, gleaming in the sunlight, was a multicolored ring with an oval stone and silver snake coiled around it. The fortune teller's ring....Valerie followed Sam's gaze. 'So I stole the ring. So what? She had no more use for it. But that doesn't mean I killed her.' Silence reigned as four pairs of accusing eyes bore into her."

We've also added a special personal touch to *Copper and Goldie*: a picture at the beginning of each story. For "The Snake Lady" it's a picture of our cousin's ring, which we show here.

Molly and the Inspector

When Larry and I started writing together, we hadn't even considered writing mysteries—until we visited my psychoanalyst father, Dr. Saul K. Pollack, in Milwaukee. That visit set us on a happy new course.

My father, a widower in his seventies, had a housekeeper/gourmet cook named Dorothy. She was sixty-three, with a beachball figure, waddle walk, honey curls, and good-natured, nosy-body personality. Dorothy had exquisite culinary skills and a unique way of expressing herself, with delicious dialogue like "I have to take my calcium so I don't get osteoferocious."

During our visit, my father pulled out a piece of paper from his desk drawer and handed it to us: his secret list of Dorothy's sayings. He thought we could submit it to *Reader's Digest*—clever, skewed expressions from a woman with only a tenth-grade education. Sometimes her malaprops were so apropos that my father wondered whether they were intentional.

We flew back home to Severna Park, and soon after, we decided Dorothy was too good a character to ignore. Forget *Reader's Digest*. She belonged to us. We named her Molly, and her witty sayings Mollyprops. But we knew she could only be half the equation, so Larry invented a driving force, a semi-retired police detective whom he named Inspector Paco LeSoto. Thus was born *Locks and Cream Cheese*, the first of our Paco and Molly Mysteries.

Character development didn't come easily. We tried the alter ego thing, but simply inserting ourselves into an observing role, no matter how engaging the plot, didn't hack it.

On the other hand, the careful melding of our semi-retired professional policeman with the curiosity-hounded housekeeper/cook did emerge in that series with a measure of success. *Locks and Cream Cheese* is our most popular mystery.

Molly Mesta's last name is a tribute to Perle Mesta, the famous Washington, D.C. hostess. A romance between Paco and Molly starts when Inspector Paco enters the home of psychoanalyst Dr. Avi Kepple—patterned after my father—to investigate a suspicious death. Cupid shoots Paco straight through the stomach with a tasty (imaginary) arrow dipped in "chocolate mousey."

Molly barges into *Locks and Cream Cheese* as the born snoop, who knows the secrets of every family member and friend of Dr. Avi. Her snooping skills prove to be of great help to Paco, and her quirky personality lends muscle to the plot. In *Locks*, just like the real-life Molly, she over-waters all the plants, leaving white rings on the elegant wood tables. She also overfeeds Dr. Avi's golden retriever, who lunches on filet mignon and scalloped potatoes. Both Dorothy and my father have passed away, but we're delighted to have immortalized them as Molly and Dr. Avi.

As Larry began inventing our Baltimore police detective, he suddenly felt he was describing someone he had known many years ago. He'd impressed Larry so much that a half-century later, Larry assigned Paco a Spanish name and began to remember where and when.

The "where" was in the port of Barcelona, Spain, and the

year was 1957. They were both dinner guests aboard a U.S. Navy ship in the harbor. He was Inspector Garcia Garcia Garcia (yeah, that's for real), a local goodwill liaison of the Barcelona *policia*. He was in his mid-fifties, short, solidly built, and nattily attired in a colorful sport coat, tie, and saddle shoes. Larry was there as a civilian global field engineer for RCA, contracted to the Navy for his skills in electronic equipment. Between dessert and coffee, the inspector and Larry found that they were the only two diners left at the table.

The inspector's command of the English language was excellent. Larry sat spellbound, listening to his endless store of police anecdotes. His dark, bushy brows and full mustache fluttered and leapt to express his words. Larry didn't realize it then, but he had benefited greatly from that meeting. The inspector became the basis for our semi-retired Baltimore homicide detective, working in the fictional Maryland town of Black Rain Corners. Paco and Molly, as endearing partners in crime, also solved cases in the next two books: *Hot Grudge Sunday* and *Boston Scream Pie*.

We've discovered a built-in problem writing about senior protagonists. Paco and Molly tended to age, right beneath our noses. In keeping with real life, we let that happen, only faster than we planned.

So we developed our younger set of sleuths for the Dan and Rivka Sherman Mysteries. They leave their professions to become owners of the Olde Victorian Bookstore—with ominous, quite sinister, consequences.

Turning a "White Elephant" into a Novel
(and the Hurdles We Faced)

*D*_{eath} *Steals A Holy Book,* our third Dan and Rivka Sherman Mystery, is based on a real-life rare book that Larry inherited. In the Preface to the novel, Larry explained it this way. "Many of us possess a "white elephant," an odd gift for which we have never found a practical or decorative place. My white elephant is the *Sefer Menorat ha-maor,* a rare, holy book passed down from my maternal grandfather to my mother and then to me."

The surprising bequest arrived in a flimsy department-store gift box nestled in tissue paper. This edition was written in Yiddish, the language that predominated among European Jews at the end of the eighteenth century when it was printed. *Sefer* means book. The English translation of *Menorat ha-maor* is *The Candlestick of Light.* It was originally written in Hebrew in the fourteenth century as a moral and religious household guide for Jews in the Middle Ages. Hugely popular in its time, it is filled with rabbinical interpretations for righteous living; a compilation of sermons, anecdotes, and tales drawn from both written and oral Jewish law and ethical teachings.

Neither Larry nor I can read Yiddish. The *Menorat ha-maor* sat on a closet shelf year after year, deteriorating. In 2008 he opened the gift box, gently lifted the book out, and placed it on the table. Small brownish flecks of the heavy leather cover fell off. Carefully opening the cover, he found neat script on the flyleaf: dates ranging from 1803 through 1836, along with names he did not recognize—probably births. The edges of the yellowed pages had turned brown as well. They were too brittle to continue in Larry's care. The cost of restoration was astronomical. Sadly, in its condition he could not display this fragile holy book in the place of honor it deserved. He sought professional advice.

After consulting a cantor and three rabbis, Larry carefully packaged up the *Menorat ha-maor* and sent it on its way to Cincinnati, Ohio, for curator evaluation. It was authenticated. Officially donated by Larry, it now resides permanently in the Rare Books collection at the venerated Klau Library of the Hebrew Union College-Jewish Institute of Religion.

The *Menorat ha-maor* inspired Larry to create the basic plot for *Death Steals A Holy Book*. Reluctant amateur sleuths Dan and Rivka yearn for a tranquil life as the owners of The Olde Victorian Bookstore in Annapolis, but when they inherit the *Menorat ha-maor,* they find themselves embroiled in a firestorm of deceit, thievery, and violence. Realizing the volume needs repair, they turn it over to Israel Finestein, renowned restorer of antique books in Baltimore. Israel has just finished his work on it when his life is brutally snuffed out and the book disappears. What makes this ancient text so valuable that someone is compelled to kill for it? Two Baltimore detectives find a puzzling number of suspects. Is it the controversial woman whom Israel plans to marry? The rare book agent who overextended himself in the stock market? Or Israel's busybody Orthodox cousins who resent his secular lifestyle?

We finished our 239-page novel, bringing the killer to justice. Intuitively, however, we knew something important was lacking. Why, we asked ourselves, should readers simply take our word for it that the *Menorat ha-maor* was a precious household guide for Jews in the Middle Ages? We knew the answer. We needed to add actual quotes from the text, one quote above each chapter heading. That would be the only way to convince readers of the antique book's value and power. Without the quotes, readers would be skeptical of the rare book's worth—and also skeptical of the motive for stealing it and murdering Israel.

But where were we going to get the quotes? We needed an English translation, and thus began our quest to locate one. We assumed it would be easy. Boy, were we wrong. For months we Googled Jewish bookstores; they offered copies in Hebrew, Yiddish, or German. Phone messages, letters, and emails to other bookstores went unanswered.

Rescue came from an unexpected source. As members of

Temple Emanu-El, we're also committee members of the temple's annual Honolulu Jewish Film Festival. On Opening Night, we were introduced to several distinguished attendees, including the chair of the Department of Classics at the University of Hawaii. That night a bell went off in my head. Maybe he could help us. The next morning we sent him an email relating our woeful tale. He immediately responded with a link to My Sefer bookstore in Brooklyn, New York. It worked! They had an English translation. The book cost $32, but we were so deliriously relieved that we paid an additional $48 for two-day shipping to Honolulu. Nothing was going to stop us from possessing this book—immediately.

After it arrived, we practically had to make appointments with each other, taking turns reading it. But we also knew we had collided with another roadblock because the title of the translation was *Menoras Hamaor*. Why was *Menorat* spelled instead with an 's'? We needed to add a paragraph to our Preface in *Death Steals A Holy Book*, explaining the anomaly this way:

"Larry's donated Yiddish copy spells *Menorat* with a 't'—the Sephardic, or Spanish, spelling. The quotes we have chosen are from the recent English translation (1982), with *Menoras* ending in 's'—the Ashkenazic, or Eastern European, spelling. Nevertheless, be assured it's the same book.—The Authors."

Death Steals A Holy Book contains thirty chapters. We needed one relevant quote for the opening page of each chapter. We spent a week choosing them. What captivated me most were the citations from the Talmud (the rabbinic teachings based on the Torah), mainly in dialogue, with interpretations and arguments staged as life-changing drama. I even found myself taking sides.

But now Larry and I faced one more major hurdle. The translation, published in 1982, is by Rabbi Yaakov Yosef Reinman. Of course it is copyrighted. Early on, we discussed our worst-case scenario. Without the rabbi's permission to reprint the quotes, we would have to remove them from the novel. Bottom line: We needed his permission. After several calls and a written request to the publisher, C.I.S., we learned that all rights had reverted to Rabbi

Reinman; they sent us his email address. We emailed him a detailed request, attaching copies of the opening page of each chapter. The next day...

"Larry!" I shouted. "Rabbi Reinman has replied!" I pirouetted around the living room. Too soon. Then I read his email. One line: "Does this book have a religious point?"

Here's Larry's reply.

"Dear Rabbi Reinman, In all honesty our book does not have a strict religious point, nor was it ever intended to. Our book is a traditional mystery, a work of fiction truly inspired by our knowledge of *Menorat ha-maor* and of our Yiddish version's eventual journey to the Klau Library. It is certainly moral and ethical in that the guilty are punished according to the laws of the land, and all religious practices mentioned are treated with respect. The quotes we selected are used to match applicable misdeeds found within the chapters. Our protagonists and several of the main characters are Jewish, ranging from Hasidic to Reform. In the last chapter Dan and Rivka announce that they will donate their copy to the Klau Library at Hebrew Union College—exactly as I did."

Our crusade ended happily. We received an immediate reply from Rabbi Reinman granting us permission and requesting a copy, which, of course, we had planned to send him.

Death Steals A Holy Book was published in 2016. These reviews convince us that, despite the hurdles we faced, we accomplished our mission of writing a compelling, original mystery.

• "Excerpts of the holy book are included at the beginning of each chapter and I was surprised how relevant some of those words of wisdom are today, such as "He who guards his mouth and tongue protects himself from woe." I enjoyed these passages, as well as the information about Jewish traditions that is included as part of the story and think the book would appeal to fans of the early works of Faye Kellerman."—**Smitten by the Book.**

• *Death Steals a Holy Book*: "Loved it!! One of the best books I have read this year. Thank you to the Milds for a really wonderful story. I will definitely be on the lookout for more of their books. Five stars!"—**Gram Tess at** *Goodreads.*

• "*Death Steals a Holy Book* is incredible and deserves a wider audience. I did not realize how prolific the two of you are – Wow! Thank you so much for this taste of your mystery literary work. Your writing IS captivating. Thank you for your wonderful (and educative) book."—**Rabbi Micah D. Greenstein**, *Senior Rabbi, Temple Israel, Memphis, Tennessee.*

• "*Death Steals a Holy Book* provides a clever plot and additional story lines, an unusual set of characters and some twists and turns. The authors provide the reader with a taste of Jewish culture and use short quotations from "The Candlestick of Life" to introduce each chapter. These touches make for a richer and more historically interesting read."—**Jane Schulz,** a former teacher, librarian, and college administrator. Citizen Reviewer, *Bismarck Tribune.*

• I love this unlikely crime fighting duo. They are wily when on the hunt for clues. They are the old couple that have been together through thick and thin and their loving relationship is obvious to the reader. The Milds have crafted these rich characters that develop more with each book. I liked them before and love them now like a couple of kooky next door neighbors.
—**Laura Hartman**@*writeknit.*

Chapter 12
MIRIAM

"I plan to sing and dance my way through life, become internationally famous and live happily ever after."
—**Miriam Luby Wolfe** in her high school yearbook

My Blogging, Tweeting Birds

At our house where I lived for forty-three years in Severna Park, Maryland, just eight miles north of Annapolis, I was an obsessive birdwatcher. So obsessive that when my daughter, Miriam, was twelve, she drew me a card with a bird on the cover and the words: "Mom, this purple polka-dotted orange-speckled sapsucker wishes you a Happy Birthday."

Three bird books crowded out the utensils in a kitchen drawer so I could identify newcomers. Spotting a new visitor made my whole day. They were always my birds, my personal friends. Once, in just two days in our backyard, I had a rare visit from an owl and saw a mommy mallard with her seven chicks parading single file across the grass. Looking out the front door I saw a hawk swoop down and catch a crow in mid-flight; and a turkey buzzard lunching on squirrel roadkill (yuck!).

One spring afternoon, I was daydreaming to avoid paying bills. As I gazed out the window above my second-floor desk, a blur of color and motion landed on every available branch of the apple tree in our backyard. The arrival of this small flock made my spine quiver. I felt a ripple of excitement because I'd never seen these lovely birds before—medium-sized, satiny, cinnamon-colored, with yellow-tipped tails, red-tipped secondary wings, smooth brown crests, and striking black masks edged in white. I thought I heard a faint soprano trill. They stayed only about ten minutes, then flew off in unison, of one mind.

Frantically paging through *A Golden Guide*, I discovered they were cedar waxwings. "Their irregular appearance makes them mystery birds. They're also voracious eaters, especially of insects and fruit." The apple tree was in transition that month. Its pink blossoms were fading and the apples had yet to arrive. If the cedar waxwings had visited a month later, they'd have stayed longer to enjoy our restaurant, maybe even picking it clean.

But the fleeting presence of that beautiful flock marked a milestone. From then on, the apple tree became a chat room. Our resident sparrows, cardinals, blue jays, mourning doves, black-capped chickadees, tufted titmice, and catbirds routinely hung out there. I heard coos, chirps, whistles, squeaks, and warbles. Were they blogging? Were they tweeting? I like to think so.

But I'm getting ahead of myself. I must tell you about the apple tree and how it came to be.

"Someday," four-year-old Miriam once told me, "I'll be able to climb all the trees I want." Looking back, her words seemed to be the beginning of a whole approach to life: that there was nothing in the world she couldn't do—and she started right in! She came home from kindergarten and announced, "Mom, there's going to be a science fair, and I'm going to grow an apple tree from a seed."

Was this even possible? I cut open a Red Delicious apple. I had no gardening expertise whatsoever, but I got some spontaneous advice from my neighbor, who was sipping coffee with me at the kitchen table. She told Miriam, "Put the seeds in warm water for two or three days first." Okaaay.

Three days later, I rustled up half a bag of potting soil from under the sink, and Miriam planted the seeds in a ceramic pot.

In a few weeks, three tiny sprouts popped up and off she went to kindergarten for the science fair. She didn't win a prize, but the tangible result was all the reward she needed. By now the sprouts were six inches high and she planted them in the backyard, near our screened porch. Despite three summers of either drought or drenching rains, our wispy apple tree struggled bravely to survive— and eventually grew bushy.

We didn't exactly plant it right. My fault. I'm impatient and didn't think to do some research before embarking on this huge quest. It developed a fat, funky, sideways-leaning trunk. Later I learned that you're supposed to graft a healthy tree cutting onto a newborn one. The tree didn't seem to care. Seven springs later, blossoms emerged like a delicate pink bonnet. And weeks later, it bore its first apples, small and green. I was ecstatic.

"Miriam, you've made yourself immortal!" But she wasn't much impressed. She was routinely adding something special to her personal history.

Miriam had just written a fan letter to Dear Abby. And another one to President Jimmy Carter, advising him on how to clean up the environment. Within a few weeks she received a thank-you from the White House signed by President Carter, and a charming hand-written note from Abby, scribbled between flights in an airport.

I discovered a remarkable coincidence. Miriam was born on September 26th. And so was John Chapman—better known as Johnny Appleseed, that marvelous pioneer who walked the countryside planting apple trees.

When I told my daughter that the apple tree made her immortal, little did I know how prophetic I was. On December 21, 1988, Miriam died in the terrorist bombing of Pan Am Flight 103 over Lockerbie, Scotland. She was twenty and my only child and Larry's stepdaughter, one of the thirty-five Syracuse University students on board, returning from a Syracuse semester in London. Larry and I had been married only thirteen months.

There is no getting over the loss of our daughter, but the

tree comforted us. During a visit by Jackie, Myrna, and our toddler grandchildren, the girls baked a delicious pie with the apples. Our last summer in Severna Park we got a healthy, abundant harvest, although Larry and I didn't normally eat the apples. When we waited until they were full-grown and red-ripe, we discovered they were holey or gouged out; the birds and worms had beaten us to them. Squirrels, too. I saw one pluck off a newborn green apple and scamper up the old maple tree outside our kitchen window, where the branches were thicker. Sitting on its haunches, the squirrel looked just like a person as it held the fruit in both paws and nibbled lunch. The apples were nurturing our local wildlife!

In 2013 Larry and I moved from Severna Park to Honolulu. We hope the buyers of our house treasure Miriam's tree as much as we did.

A longer version of "My Blogging, Tweeting Birds" was performed by the Petaluma (California) Readers Theatre in September 2011 with photos of Miriam and her apple tree.

Joy, Light, and Love

At our house on Christmas Day, 1988, somebody switched on the TV. Anxious family members clustered in our living room. A cereal commercial blared. Then the kindly face of Charles Kuralt filled the screen to broadcast his usual *Sunday Morning* program. That Sunday morning he devoted his program to Pan Am Flight 103, including an interview with a State Department expert on counterterrorism.

Suddenly, an amazing thing happened. Mr. Kuralt finished his program with these words:

"It is hard to think of large numbers of disaster victims as individuals, but we should try. We received this letter just before Christmas. It comes to us from Kenneth Bolinsky of Sellersville,

Pennsylvania. It says:

'Dear Mr. Kuralt: In the folklore of Eastern European Jewry is found the tale of the Tzaddikim—thirty-six holy good souls upon whose existence lies the responsibility for the balance of good and evil in the universe. The Tzaddik is, however, totally unaware of this burden. I am writing to tell you of one such soul. During my three years of graduate study at Syracuse University she became a part of my days—a soothing moment in passing. She was a blissfully talented creature full of joy and of light and of love. She was my friend. There is now a serious imbalance in the universe: Miriam Wolfe was aboard Pan Am Flight 103. I thought you'd want to know.'"

Of *all* the passengers on the plane, it was my daughter whom Mr. Kuralt chose to talk about. I asked myself whether I had understood my child too little; whether I had paid too little attention. In April, 1989 I wrote Ken Bolinsky to thank him. Here was his reply:

"Dear Mr. and Mrs. Mild: I got to know Miriam through other friends: I chose to share their grief at her loss, not recognizing my own. We are a strange animal, not always knowing when we have been wounded and, even then, not how deeply. I wrote the letter to Mr. Kuralt out of a sense of fear, of emptiness—I had to share my anxiety. The writing was my catharsis. I cannot tell you why I sent the letter to him—I'm not certain that I know. Perhaps because I have come to trust him. I marked it 'Personal' and never expected a response in any form. I heard the words I had written while preparing my family's Christmas breakfast and found myself crying again. What followed, though, was something wonderful. As the broadcast made its way across the country, distant friends called to share their frustration at the horror that had befallen us all. Miriam allowed us to touch, and ease, our mutual pain. How like her to help others, to help strangers find a healing peace. Perhaps that is the memory of your daughter that stays with me: I keep it like a smooth, bright pebble—safe in the bottom of a pocket."

Tulips on Trial

When you plant tulip bulbs in October, you take a lot on faith. Will they reward you with gorgeous blooms in the spring? Or will the squirrels get there first, burrowing in, digging up the bulbs, and feasting on them?

For Larry and me, this endeavor was akin to buying a lottery ticket. We're not clever gardeners. Nevertheless, my fragile hopes ran high in October, 2000, when we diligently planted fifty bulbs in the modest flower bed fronting our house. We bought our pack of bulbs in Alsmeer, the Netherlands, home of the largest flower auction in the world. But these were not your ordinary bulbs. Our precious tulips came fraught with symbolism and represented a grievous journey.

We bought them a week before traveling to Kamp Zeist, southeast of Amsterdam. We were headed there to attend the trial of the two Libyan terrorists, Abdel Basset al-Megrahi and Lamen Khalifa Fhimah. They were indicted by the United States and Great Britain in 1991 for the bombing of Pan Am Flight 103.

In the Alsmeer gift shop, as I waited to pay for our bulbs, my thoughts drove me down two avenues: the romance of buying tulips in Holland and their emotional context on the eve of the trial. These captivating flowers would be more than a souvenir. They would stand, year after year, as a memorial to Miriam.

So stubbornly had I fixed on these profound implications that I neglected to ask the gift shop ladies just where it is that you plant tulip bulbs. In the shade? In full sun?

Larry and I learned the answer by default. Across the street from our house, the sunny side, our neighbors' tulips bloom weeks before ours. Oh, dear. Tulips belong in full sun. We, on the north side, get only half-sun. Sometimes only quarter-sun. In the winter, snow sits on our front lawn longer than on anyone else's in the neighborhood.

In mid-April, 2001, the first bud popped open. I leaned over it and stared in dismay. So skinny. Would they all be like that?

Do tulip blossoms get larger, more robust each day? Or, if they're born underdeveloped, do they stay pathetic, unable to catch up? Amazingly enough, each day new blooms greeted me. And with each one, I rushed back into the house and announced their status to Larry. "We have seven, dear. Come look!" I shouted. "We're up to twelve!" I cheered. I counted the blooms obsessively at least once a day.

Our fifty brave bulbs gave birth to sixty-four blooms. And they all progressed to a hearty cup shape. Not earth-shattering, not prize-winning, but respectable. I took pictures to capture their beauty: a blaze of yellow bursting inside a scarlet cup; a white star nestling in velvety purple. Each day as I bounded out of the house for the morning paper, I greeted our tulips as if they'd be with me forever.

* * * *

The trial of the two Libyans took place in the Netherlands before a Scottish court at Kamp Zeist, a former American Air Force base. The United Nations had negotiated this unusual arrangement with Libyan leader Moammar Gadhafi, who demanded that the trial be held in a neutral country. A concrete building at Kamp Zeist was transformed into a modern courthouse with a special secluded lounge for the victims' families. We attended the trial— already in its sixth month—for a week in October, 2000, along with twelve other Pan Am family members. Before leaving for Europe, I cried for days, filled with anxiety over the prospect of facing the murderers of my daughter. Nevertheless, Larry and I realized there would be a cathartic benefit to seeing them in the flesh and showing our support for their prosecution.

Our first morning, as our minibus approached the courthouse, we saw formidable but reassuring security. High chain-link fences with barbed wire. Scottish guards in blue, white, and black uniforms with Kevlar vests and automatic weapons. Entering the courtroom for the first time sent a chill down my spine. A massive, floor-to-ceiling bulletproof glass wall separated the spectators from the court itself. Just beyond the glass, on the left, the defendants

191

sat in an elevated box flanked by two guards. Directly below them, the defense team occupied two rows of tables and chairs. Facing them along the right wall was the Crown's prosecution team, as well as several U.S. State Department advisers. The three presiding judges, plus one alternate, occupied the "bench," a massive raised dais under the Scottish court crest.

I stared at the two men accused of mass murder, the men who had destroyed the life of my beautiful Miriam. A wave of fear shot through me. Not because they looked like monsters, not because I felt physically threatened. But because they looked so ordinary. Author Hannah Arendt, writing about Nazi war criminal Adolph Eichmann, described "the banality of evil." I had not understood the concept before. Now I did.

The spectator side of the glass wall held upholstered theater-style chairs with headphones available for translations. We family members were seated in the large center section near the front. The physical closeness of these twelve warm, loving people—strangers to Larry and me before the trial—gave me strength. We shared so much, belonging to an involuntary club as victims of terrorism. We shared memories of our loved ones; the pain of our altered lives; our feelings toward the accused; the splintered and sometimes biased media; and the sway of the trial itself.

At the back of the courtroom sat a group of special observers of varying ethnic origins, representing the United Nations War Crimes Commission. The defendants' families and supporters, numbering only a few, occupied the smaller section on the left. My eyes unwillingly met the angry gaze of a large swarthy woman wearing the traditional black head scarf: the terrorist Megrahi's wife. Her outfit, a long print skirt and jacket, could have come from Sears or J.C. Penney. She sat with their two children, perhaps pre-teens, who fidgeted in their chairs. A stream of heavy emotions tugged at me. *The defendants have families? Loved ones? Could men so zealously evil, deliberately killing innocents, even babies, have genuine feelings? Doesn't ice water run in their veins?*

We were all warned to use only the restrooms in our family

lounge, not the general one for all trial visitors out in the corridor, because we might find ourselves in a confrontation.

It is widely believed that Scotland is one of the most pro-defendant countries in the world. The *Washington Post* reported that a special chef would prepare meals for the two defendants. The court also granted them a prayer room and exercise room. Did Oklahoma City bombers Timothy McVeigh and Terry McNichols—or any other mass murderer in an American prison—ever receive such amenities?

JANUARY 31, 2001: The three Scottish judges pronounced Megrahi "Guilty!" and sentenced him to twenty years before he would be eligible for parole—the longest sentence allowed under Scottish law. We family members were outraged and frustrated. It was quickly pointed out that a sentence of twenty years meant Megrahi would serve less than one month for each of the 270 victims. Adding to our dismay, Fhimah was declared "Not guilty." The prosecution could not directly link him to the purchase of the timer circuit board that triggered the bomb. We felt sick to read that he flew home to a hero's welcome. Nevertheless, a small measure of gratitude swept over Larry and me. At least we got one conviction. Evil had not won out entirely. Most of the families felt as we did. Nothing would bring our children back, but after twelve years, the verdict gave us a particle of justice. Our sense of gratitude did not last long. As for peace of mind? Forget it. Here's why.

SEPTEMBER 11, 2001: Xian, China, on our Grand Circle tour. Larry and I awoke early, still tasting the exhilaration of our previous day's visit to the vast building housing the terra cotta warriors. The phone rang. It was Marty, our friend and fellow traveler in the hotel room next door. "Turn on CNN!" he shouted.

The terrorist attacks on American soil had changed our world for the worst—again. Shock waves and fear reverberated through our tour group. Frantic phone calls from a wife to a husband working in the Pentagon. A son on Wall Street. Grandchildren in western Pennsylvania. Our fellow travelers knew how my daughter died and whispered among themselves: "How's Rosemary? Is she okay?"

Outwardly, yes, I was calm. Too calm. In fact, at first I felt almost nothing. My brain shifted into reverse, disconnecting me from reality. To make things worse, the Chinese government took CNN off the air. The full impact of 9/11 stubbornly escaped me. We were halfway around the world, not in our kitchen in Severna Park, inches from the phone and the cold Pan Am voice that told me, at 12:30 a.m. on December 22, 1988: "M. Wolfe is on the manifest."

During the following days, the enormity of the 9/11 attacks seeped in. Our tour ended in Hong Kong. Inside the airport, tall Chinese soldiers patrolled with automatic weapons poised, ready to fire. A spasm cramped my belly—not from the vicious abdominal cramps that my Crohn's disease often inflicted, but from a sense of hopelessness and dread. Even today I feel haunted, thinking of the hundreds of brave firefighters and other heroic souls who perished trying to save lives during the destruction of the Twin Towers, the Pentagon, and Flight 93.

The Pan Am 103 families had spearheaded a potent new law, the Aviation Security Improvement Act of 1990. Was it all for nothing? For centuries, philosophers have warned that those who ignore history are doomed to repeat it. How could the United States Government have failed so miserably to anticipate 9/11?

Michael Chertoff became the first Secretary of the Department of Homeland Security, created in 2002 in response to 9/11. He has provided some cogent answers. Every December 21, a commemoration service is held at the Pan Am 103 memorial cairn in Arlington National Cemetery, in Arlington, Virginia. On December 21, 2007, then-Secretary Chertoff was the keynote speaker and said:

"The sad truth is that what followed Lockerbie was not a period of sober remembrance and reappraisal. What followed Lockerbie was a time of tremendous amnesia and self-delusion. Less than a year after Lockerbie, the Berlin Wall came down and two years later, the Soviet Union fell and hundreds of millions of people were liberated from the tyranny of Communism. As the world rightly celebrated, Lockerbie was all but forgotten. There was even talk about the end of history, but columnist Charles Krauthammer got it right when he said that in the years that followed, we took a 'holiday from history.' The terrorists, however, took no such holiday, but worked overtime to launch future attacks. In 1993, they bombed the World Trade Center. By the mid-Nineties, they had almost succeeded in blowing up the Lincoln and Holland tunnels. In 1996, they attacked our forces in Khobar Towers [Saudi Arabia]. In 1998, ten years after Lockerbie, Osama Bin Laden openly declared war, commanding his followers 'to kill the Americans and their allies—civilian and military—in any country where it is possible to do it.' And then came the African Embassy bombings, the USS Cole attack, and finally, September 11th. By choosing the primrose path of complacency borne out of euphoria, by forgetting the horror of Lockerbie, and by failing to respond fully to the evil done that day, we arrived at the deadly destination of September 11, 2001."

THE APPEAL: When you lose a child, there's no such thing as closure—not for me, anyway. But with the verdict of "Guilty!" at Kamp Zeist, I naively assumed we had arrived at legal closure. I should have known better. Megrahi launched his appeal immediately. But first came a hearing to decide whether the appeal should be allowed to go forward.

Back home in Severna Park, Larry and I followed the proceedings on the secure website established for the Flight 103 families by the U.S. Department of Justice Office for Victims of Crime. Each day, as we printed out summaries of the hearing, I agonized over every shred of the defense's arguments.

On October 15, 2001, the five new Scottish judges announced their decision. I was horrified and ranted to Larry: "It's only a month after 9/11! How can they allow the appeal to go forward?" I paced the kitchen floor, my voice strident. "The trial lasted nine months and the Libyans had eleven years to prepare their case. Why is Megrahi being given such leeway? It's shameful!"

My husband had no answer.

The appeal trial lasted thirteen months. As we read the summaries each day, Larry remained coolly confident that each new piece of "evidence" produced in such volume by the defense was flimsy. I agreed with him intellectually, but my stomach knotted up with doubt. What if the conviction was overturned? What if no one was made to pay for Miriam's death?

On March 14, 2002, at 5:30 a.m. Eastern Standard Time, the five Scottish judges announced their verdict: "We have concluded that none of the grounds of the appeal is well founded. The appeal will accordingly be refused. This brings proceedings to an end."

At the time, Larry and I were spending the winter in Hawaii. Holding our breath, our eyes transfixed on CNN, we heard the verdict. Appeal denied. We did not whoop and cheer. No. We fell into each other's arms and wept.

I could breathe again. But I still felt a lurking reserve—until much later that day, when I logged onto the *New York Times* online and read "Megrahi was flown to Scotland late tonight to begin his sentence there." That single line somehow liberated me, released me. It was the first tangible news, something I could grasp and clutch and cling to. Megrahi was now physically caged in a Victorian-era prison in Glasgow. According to Reuters news service, Barlinnie has borne the reputation (until recently) as Scotland's toughest jail, administered under "Dickensian conditions." Yes! The bomber was being punished for his unspeakable mass murder of 270 innocent victims.

Megrahi, the former security chief of Libyan Arab Airlines in Malta, is of course only one man. Although Fhimah was acquitted, the U.S. Government believes he, too, was guilty. And it is universally known that the two men did not act on their own, that the order to bomb Pan Am 103 came from Gadhafi himself. For many years, Libya was known to sponsor terrorism.

A civil suit that had been filed by a group of Pan Am 103 families against Libya was now settled. The civil action included the cornerstone condition that Moammar Gadhafi take public responsibility for the bombing and renounce terrorism. In 2003, under pressure from the United States, Great Britain, and the United Nations, he renounced his country's terrorism and agreed to dismantle his nuclear weapons program. In 2005, at last, Libya accepted responsibility for the bombing of Pan Am 103.

We returned home from Hawaii in time for our darling tulips to perform for another season. As we wheeled our luggage up the walk, I cheered. "Larry, they're coming up!"

Well, sort of. A few scrawny leaves greeted us. In the next few weeks, I expected them to burst forth with buds and blooms even stronger and healthier than the first year's. I expected them to join Larry and me in celebrating and symbolizing our victory.

But April and May came and went. In our entire flower bed, only twelve clumps of leaves appeared. Twelve clumps. Not one tulip! There the leaves stood: lonely, straggly, disheartened. And surrounding them, I discovered dents in the soil. Dents and deep holes. Larry leaned down and studied them. "Hmm," he said. "Must be the squirrels." I nodded, too disappointed to agree aloud.

Several years ago, we planted gerbera daisies and the flowers popped out in blazing yellows, oranges and purples. By the next morning, each dazzling bloom had disappeared. Rabbits had devoured them for breakfast. After a week of this, I got so frustrated that I sped across the highway to our local garden center and bought a bunch of silk roses, complete with fake dew on their delicate petals. Our friends raved about our stunning roses. Until they tried to smell them.

So...after a day of pondering the dents in the garden, I could visualize what must have happened. Our squirrels undoubtedly followed the Libyans' trial and appeal. In my mind's eye, I could see them gathered in a huddle, their plumed tales quivering.

"Listen up," the head honcho squirrel said. "The trial's over. The appeal's over. Let's eat!"

My daughter had an unquenchable optimism and vision— far greater than my own—to explore her talents, to soak up experiences, and to seek out new ones. In a paper she wrote at Syracuse, she said, "To be a true artist, one must challenge and defy convention, remain open-minded, and always continue to learn."

It's time to take my cue from Miriam. Instead of brooding about spring blooms and what will come up or not come up, I think of our precious Dutch bulbs and pack them away in a corner of my memory. I smile at the squirrels prancing along our maple branches. My decision is made. I jump in my car and head for the garden center. I hear they have exquisite silk tulips.

Not Over Yet

On December 21st, 2020, the U.S. Department of Justice charged a third Libyan accomplice in the bombing of Pan Am Flight 103. Abu Agila Mas'ud, a bomb-making expert in the employ of the former Libyan intelligence agency, was charged with two criminal counts related to the bombing. Mas'ud is currently in Libyan custody. U.S. Attorney General William Barr said U.S. officials are hopeful that Libya will allow Mas'ud to be tried in the United States. Mas'ud was alleged to be the one who made the bomb and carried it from Libya to Malta in a suitcase and then set the timer. Ironically, the charges came thirty-two years to the day that my daughter was taken from me.

Surviving in Spite of...

Losing a child is the ultimate hell. There is no getting over it. So much love, so much potential destroyed.

Months later, after the dust of anguish and denial settled around me, I began my first memoir about her and called it *Miriam's Gift: A Mother's Blessings—Then and Now*. My introduction described her accomplishments—at the remarkable age of twenty—as an actress, singer, dancer, writer, director, and teacher. But the tone seemed wrong. It was too cool, too reportorial. I'd been a career editor and free-lancer, writing profiles of other people for so many years that I didn't know how to write from my gut.

One night Larry handed me three sheets of paper. He had spent his lunch hour at work writing an introduction to my memoir. I read it in shock. It plumbed the depths of sorrow without embarrassment. And without gushing, he described Miriam's legacy as a passionate friend who enriched the life of everyone who met her. I finally understood. I needed to uncork my bottled emotions— anger and grief, love and guilt. Telling the truth meant admitting my weaknesses as a harried, divorced mother; allowing Miriam to be human; and daring to inject the darkest humor. The most dramatic example: All six of our pets croaked within six months of my divorce! Oh, boy. It wasn't enough that I hadn't disciplined Miriam enough growing up. I was also an atrocious pet owner. Is there a message here? Did one impact the other?

The reality of losing Miriam stings today as much today as it did the day she died. One of the first questions I asked myself was, *If I've lost my only child am I still a mother?* Yes, I'll always be her mother. And I'm a stepmother, too.

Now, thirty-two years later, I have never gotten past the reality of learning about Miriam's friends' lives. All married. With children, and their family photos. Back then I had no idea what would be confronting me on a daily basis. One Sunday morning, in the Giant produce department in Severna Park, I bumped into an acquaintance from temple. She was agitated and regurgitated her distress to me as if I were her closest buddy. "My daughter is dating a man twenty years older with teenage children." I yearned to say, "Get over it. As least you *have* a daughter to worry about."

Even my best friend threw me a curve ball. " 'Sally' broke her toe. That child is so clumsy!" I gritted my teeth, got off the phone, and paced across the kitchen floor ranting to Larry. "How could she tell me that? It's so petty, so insensitive." Larry tried to reason with me. "Actually," he said, "she loved Miriam and she loves you, too. It's something you'll always be facing. Your friends are going to talk about their children." A few months later the subject of Sally's toe came up over lunch. My best friend confessed,

"When I hung up that day I wished I hadn't told you about it."

So what keeps me going? Overriding the never-ending sense of loss is the love and loyalty shown by her friends. How can I not be proud and touched that two of them (and my cousin) named their children after her? Three middle names, and her best friend, Wendy, naming her fourth child Miriam. And all her friends remember her on Facebook, bringing me to tears of gratitude, with photos and memories on her birthday and on December 21. Pictures of Miriam are permanently on Wendy's Facebook pages, group photos of all the girls having a wonderful time together. And her devoted friend Jake posted his superb essay about her on Facebook with a joyous photo of the two of them in London.

I received an unexpected gift from the Scottish police. They were able to return most of Miriam's things to me. Among them were her writings: poems, essays, and diaries. I had no idea she was so prolific. So, burrowing into her closet I made more astonishing discoveries: folders filled with short stories and poems composed in her sophomore-year creative writing class. I jubilantly published many of the writings in the *Washington Post, Cricket, Soap Opera Stars, Dramatics Magazine, Kids' Byline, Art Times*, and elsewhere. With every publication I felt I had immortalized her. But my exhilaration didn't stop there.

I published my first memoir, *Miriam's Gift*, in 1999. Ten years later, when I told friends and family I was considering writing a sequel, some of them groaned. Others said, "LET IT GO!" They were all too polite to physically walk away from me, but I could feel the negative aura. Like they were walking out of a bad three-act play after the first act.

But I'm not good at taking advice. Ask Larry. I just barreled on, reasoning that *Miriam's Gift* ended before the two bombers had even been apprehended. I shouted out, "Wait, there's more!" So *Miriam's World—and Mine* was born. After approaching several commercial publishers without success, I decided *Okay, to heck with them, I'll do it myself*, and I happily included a special section for all of Miriam's best writings. The nuggets of *Miriam's Gift* are still there, but tightened, shortened, more intense, with lots of important new material: the capture of the bombers, the trial, the prison term, and most outrageous of all, the British/Libyan sinister deal-making. (It's all in the *Miriam's World—and Mine* chapter "270 Betrayals.")

I had an enlightening conversation with an extended family member, who lost her twenty-three-year-old daughter, her only child, to an illness. I asked Vicky, "Do you miss her?" Vicky replied, "No, because she's always with me."

I can relate to that. My most precious moments are the snippets of memories that reside in my head as if Miriam were still with me. Here are a few.

• Sometimes she blew me away with her maturity—the wisdom of an adult. I was selling real estate and told her, "I have to be extra careful with this contract. The buyer is a state trooper." In a world-weary voice at age ten, she said, "Oh, Mom, he's just a person like everybody else." Selling real estate turned out to be a 24/7 job—not exactly ideal when you've just separated from your husband who had done a lot of babysitting. I got rejected by twenty teenage sitters for a Saturday in June; they were all busy. *Harrumph!* Next best thing: Take Miriam with me to an appointment. I had lectured her in the car about being totally quiet. In vain. My customer was a reserved, no-nonsense type, a serious buyer looking for a large, posh house. We entered the marble-floored foyer. In a flash, Miriam darted up the curved staircase and called out, "Wait till you see the master bedroom!" I thought it was rather funny. She had learned the vocabulary from listening to me on the phone. My customer was not amused. She was the mother of eight undoubtedly well-behaved children. Surprisingly, I made the sale anyway.

• With a fourth-grade friend over, she dragged the mattress off our guest-room daybed, and they used use it as a toboggan to slide down the thirteen stairs into the living room.

• Shortly after I separated, Miriam had her favorite neighborhood friend over. They were playing upstairs. I was in the living room reading, not realizing they were in the second-floor guest bathroom making bubbles in the sink with Softsoap. Suddenly, I heard giggles and splashing sounds. I rushed upstairs. The girls had filled the sink with water and splashed it around jubilantly—until it overflowed with soapy puddles all over the pink-tiled floor. If only I'd been paying attention.

• One Saturday night I allowed her to go to the movies with three friends who lived in Severna Park. But it was nearly midnight. Where was she? I paced the living room floor. At one a.m. they finally dropped her off. She came rushing in the door, flushed with excitement and laughter.

"Mom! You won't believe what we did. Austin's family has a canoe. We went canoeing at midnight! Such a great time!"

I guess Miriam was at her most mischievous, her way of protesting, because of the breaking-up of my marriage. That's when I started to learn some single-parent skills, like how to replace a three-foot section of screening on our back porch. Miriam and her friend Judy had walked over to our house from hers and entered through the back door on our porch. Judy's Great Dane puppy had been loose in her yard and, unbeknownst to the girls, followed them to our house. The girls and I were in the kitchen when we heard a *Crash!* The puppy wasn't to be denied. He plunged through a three-foot panel on the porch, expecting to join us in the house.

• Grandpa Saul called often from Milwaukee. With his wry sense of humor, he would ask: "So, Miriam, how's it going in Reform School?" And she'd reply in her most serious junior-high voice, "Well, Grandpa, in my time off for good behavior I'm doing a little acting."

• She took forever to get ready for school, even though I begged her to lay out her clothes the night before. Once she told me she wished they had uniforms in high school so she wouldn't have to constantly decide what to wear. One morning, not the first time she missed the school bus, I had to drive her to school. Trying to cross Ritchie Highway in heavy rush-hour traffic and get us there without an accident was a real challenge. Her reaction: "Mom, I know why you're driving so slow. It's to teach me a lesson!"

For me, slow was a slow burn.

    • When Larry and I were at Syracuse for the first Pan Am memorial gathering, a friend of Miriam's spoke to me at lunch. During sophomore year, Kim and Miriam had been talking about art, and Kim confessed that she didn't like Picasso. "Miriam jumped all over me. 'You don't like Picasso?' I just shrank away." I smiled ruefully, totally getting it. My daughter had an aggressive streak, not always charming, borne of strong convictions. I wonder whether she actually got it from me.

    • Once she complained, "Mom, you can't say anything to me without lecturing." At the time I replied, "That's my mission in life: to teach you." Looking back, I'm thinking, *Whoa, I was supposed to be listening.* Bad mother! Knowing myself, if I were starting out all over again, I'd probably do the same thing.

Miriam had a joyful personality and her optimism sustains me every hour of my life. Among her things returned to me by the Scottish police was a little journal she kept on a trip to Wales. Sitting on a hillside overlooking Kidwelly Castle, she wrote at the end of her first day:

"The sky was bluer today, the sun was yellower today, and the whole of the earth seemed to be rejoicing in its own perfection."

It Gives Me Great Strength

I find great comfort in the three annual Maryland scholarships in Miriam's memory:
    • Severna Park High School: The Miriam Luby Wolfe
        Memorial English Award.
    • Children's Theatre of Annapolis: Two Miriam Luby
        Wolfe Scholarships each year.
    • Temple Beth Shalom, Arnold, Maryland. The Miriam
        Luby Wolfe Scholarships.
I always contribute an autographed copy of my second

memoir to each recipient, as well as a personal letter, saying: "….In 2013 Larry and I moved to Honolulu, Hawaii. Presenting the award in person was always a milestone event for me. Even so far away it gives me great strength to know that Miriam's values and ideals are being carried on by such deserving students."

The Syracuse University Remembrance Scholars Program provides thirty-five large scholarships at the end of the recipients' junior year in memory of each of the thirty-five Syracuse students lost aboard Pan Am 103. The 2019 recipient in Miriam's memory was Dina Eldawy. She wrote this inspiring letter to Larry and me:

"I've wanted to be a Remembrance Scholar ever since I first applied to Syracuse. I'm a Muslim and an Arab woman so the topic of terrorism has marked my life in ways I felt I could not control. I felt an overwhelming need to humanize myself and change the narrative surrounding terrorism to stop spreading fear and hatred and rather focus on interfaith, intercultural unity. I'm studying International Relations...and Citizenship & Civic Engagement, which allows me to work with refugees in Syracuse."

Every fall SU holds a Remembrance Week, including a Rose Laying Ceremony at the Pan Am memorial. Each scholarship recipient lays a rose on the victim's name and makes a small speech: "I am laying this rose for Miriam….We remember her…for her talent, passion, and fascination with the world around her."

Comfort in Cloth: The Remembrance Quilt

The 1998 Remembrance Scholars met to decide on a fitting memorial to mark the tenth year (I hate the word anniversary) of the bombing of Pan Am 103. Without having the slightest idea of the immensity of the project—and less than two months to produce it—they decided to create a Remembrance Quilt.

All the Pan Am families received letters inviting them to send mementoes to be included in the quilt. I was so exhilarated that I felt like shipping Miriam's entire room to them because I had so much to share. What I finally chose were the photo of her that I used for the cover of *Miriam's Gift*; her silver seagull pin—she had a passion for the Chesapeake Bay; one of her favorite earrings; and a photo of her with her stepbrother, Chris Spencer. I also included the last paragraph of Miriam's letter to Chris on how to apply to college: "Do what's best for you. Your parents will love you no matter what. And so will I. I am sooo proud of you."

What takes my breath away even today is not only the skill, but the love and tenderness revealed by those who worked day and night to create this memorial. A flood of volunteers in the SU community—and the city of Syracuse—came forward, especially quilting groups. So did many eager individuals, including a janitor who wanted to stitch the block for a boy from his hometown.

Each block is about the size of a standard sheet of paper (8.5 by 11 inches). The quilt's finished size is seven square feet! A large center panel is based on an illustration created in 1989 by an SU art student: a dove of peace, formed by the students' names. The thirty-five blocks, arranged alphabetically by last name, are individual commemorations. A local sewing store embroidered the students' names on the blue lattice beneath the blocks.

The Remembrance Scholars (bless their hearts!) added other appropriate symbols to each block. Those for Miriam include a stack of books; a musical staff; and the song title "Memory" from *Cats,* which she loved to sing. Miriam and I had attended *Cats* together at the National Theatre in Washington, D.C. The day before, we read T.S. Eliot's *Old Possum's Book of Practical Cats*, on which the show is based. We found it astonishing that the lyrics followed the poems almost word for word. And when the tattered Grizabella sang "Memory" we held hands and cried.

The Remembrance Quilt traveled for display to Lockerbie and to many U.S. cities. It was on display at a hotel in Washington during an official briefing for Pan Am families by Attorney General Janet Reno, who graciously spoke with each of us personally after the briefing. I presented her with an autographed copy of *Miriam's Gift*. Later that day, family members saw her studying the quilt, and I noticed her actually looking at Miriam's block.

A poster of the quilt hangs in our Honolulu living room.

Syracuse University
REMEMBRANCE QUILT

HONORING THE VICTIMS OF PAN AM 103

10th Anniversary • December 21,1998

Miriam's patch on the Remembrance Quilt
(Seated on the bench she's with her stepbrother, Chris Spencer.)

"This Day Is Mine"

In October, 1993 I reached a milestone. I published an article in *McCall's* entitled "Please Remember My Daughter." The day of publication gave me a sense of achievement like no other since she died. Now millions of readers throughout the world knew about my child.

The article ended with Miriam's own words, her personal guidelines for her life. The force of her personality came through with such power that the response to the article surprised even me. A high school senior in Maryland concluded her graduation valedictory address with Miriam's words. A woman in Israel invited Larry and me to visit. A teacher in Ohio called to say Miriam's story had given her courage and strength—strength that she sorely needed, because this single Caucasian woman had adopted an African-American baby and most of her family had disowned her afterward.

The editor-in-chief of *McCall's*, Kate White (now editor-in-chief of *Cosmopolitan*), wrote to me on September 19, 1993. "Reading about Miriam has had a very big effect on my life—I really carry her wisdom with me every day now. I had gotten away from seeing the joy of each day and she has restored my spirit. What a fabulous legacy."

What were Miriam's words that stoked the fires of so many people? They were her own prescription for living, her personal philosophy, which I myself only discovered in one of her London notebooks. It is such profound advice that it speaks to all of us. But it speaks especially to me. With these words, my daughter has taken me by the hand and led me into a healing place.

"There are times when the 'poor me' mood is upon us; we're overwhelmed by all the troubles we have to face. This is especially likely to happen when we have begun to try to change our thinking about ourselves and our relation to others. We may, at first, become too analytical and try to solve too much at once. For this frame of mind there is an almost infallible prescription: to empty our minds of all thoughts but one—today and how to use it. This day is mine. It is unique. Nobody in the world has one exactly like it. It holds the sum of all my past experience and all my future potential."

—Miriam

Miriam and Rosemary in her SU dorm sophmore year.

Miriam aboard ship on the way to the Netherlands
during her junior semester abroad.

**My three girls. With me from left: Jackie Mild Lau, Myrna Mild
Spurrier (receiving her Master's in Education), and Miriam.**

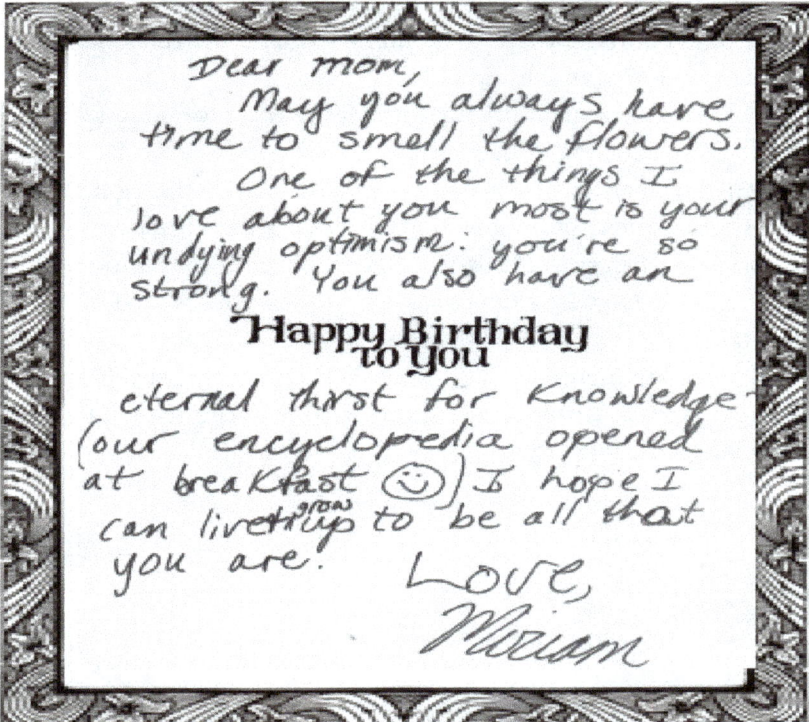

Dear mom,
     May you always have
time to smell the flowers.
     One of the things I
love about you most is your
undying optimism: you're so
strong. You also have an

**Happy Birthday
to you**

eternal thirst for knowledge
(our encyclopedia opened
at breakfast ☺) I hope I
can live/grow up to be all that
you are.
                    Love,
                    Miriam

Miriam's card for my 50th birthday. She was 17.

"To hope is normal, to expect is naïve"—wise advice that Rosemary Mild's psychoanalyst father taught her, and which she too often ignores.

Rosemary is an award-winning writer of personal essays that have appeared in the *Washington Post, Baltimore Sun, Chess Life, Generations,* and elsewhere. As a retired career editor, she's a long-time member of the Society of Professional Journalists and was a Silver Owl (twenty-five-year member) of the National Press Club in Washington, D.C. Rosemary grew up in Milwaukee and graduated from Smith College. In 2013, she and Larry moved to Honolulu, Hawaii, where they cherish time with their daughter, son-in-law, and grandchildren.

When not dreaming up outrageous ideas for her essays, she and Larry wallow in crimes and clues as coauthors of more than a dozen mystery and suspense novels and story collections. They have short stories in four anthologies: *Chesapeake Crimes: Homicidal Holidays; Mystery in Paradise; Dark Paradise;* and new in January, 2021: *Kissing Frogs and Other Quirky Tales*—spoofs of traditional fairy tales.

They're members of Mystery Writers of America, Sisters in Crime (Larry's a Mister), and Hawaii Fiction Writers. Visit them at **www.magicile.com.**

The Paco and Molly
Mystery Series (#1)

Locks and Cream Cheese—In scandal-ridden Black Rain Corners, a Chesapeake Bay mansion harbors locked rooms and deadly secrets. A wily detective and a gourmet cook tackle the case.

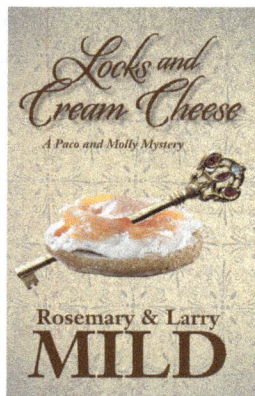

The Paco and Molly
Mystery Series (#2)

Hot Grudge Sunday—Bank robbers and conspirators derail the sleuths' blissful honeymoon at the Grand Canyon. Can they nail the suspects after they themselves become targets?

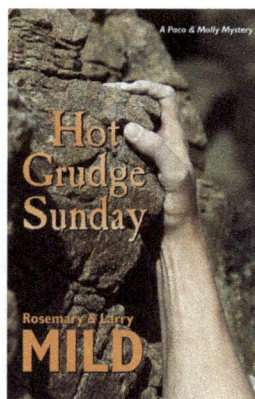

The Paco and Molly
Mystery Series (#3)

Boston Scream Pie—A teenage girl's nightmare triggers a sinister tale of twins, two feuding families, and a blonde bombshell who hates being called "Mom."

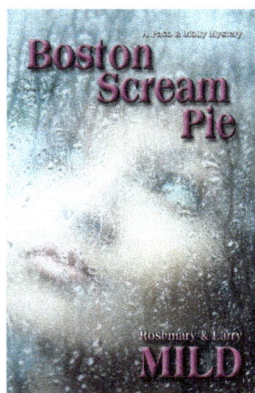

Available on Amazon.com and all e-readers.

The Dan and Rivka Sherman Mystery Series (#1)

Death Goes Postal—Rare 15th-century typesetting artifacts journey through time, leaving a horrifying imprint in their wake. Dan and Rivka risk life and limb to locate the treasures and unmask the murderer. Not quite what they expected when they bought The Olde Victorian Bookstore. (**Also available as an Amazon Audible Audiobook**.)

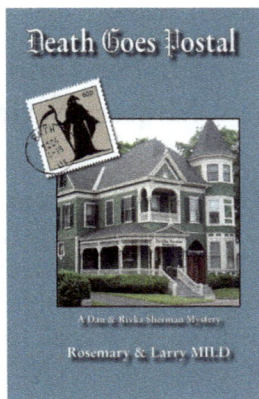

The Dan and Rivka Sherman Mystery Series (#2)

Death Takes A Mistress—A young Englishwoman is murdered by her lover. Years later, her daughter, seeking revenge, journeys from London to Annapolis, MD to find the killer and her father. But to which family does he belong? Dan and Rivka set out to expose the true villain.

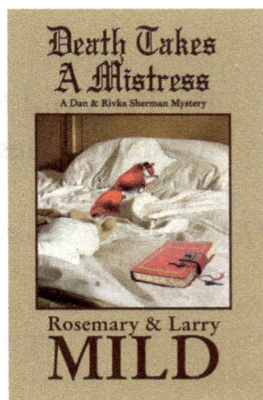

The Dan and Rivka Sherman Mystery Series (#3)

Death Steals A Holy Book—Dan and Rivka inherit a rare Yiddish translation of a 14th-century holy book, but it is stolen and their book restorer is murdered. Can they recover the book and nail the culprit?

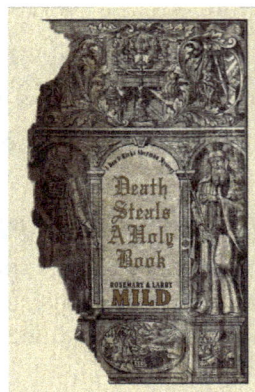

Available on Amazon.com and all e-readers.

The Dan and Rivka Sherman Mystery Series (#4)

Death Rules the Night—Dan wants to know why all copies of an important book are missing, not only from the bookstore, but also from all the local libraries and the author's bookshelves. Who is trying to hide the book's secrets and what are they? Can stalking, threats, and even murder sway Dan from solving this mystery? Rivka fears for their lives.

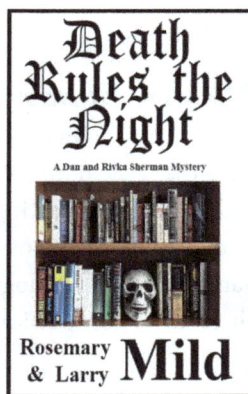

Cry Ohana, Adventure and Suspense in Hawaii—A car accident, blackmail, and murder tear apart a Hawai'ian *ohana* (family). Kekoa, the teenage son, witnesses the murder and is forced into life on the run. Danger erupts at a Filipino wedding, a Maui resort, and the Big Island's volcanic steam vents. Can the family re-unite and bring down the killer?

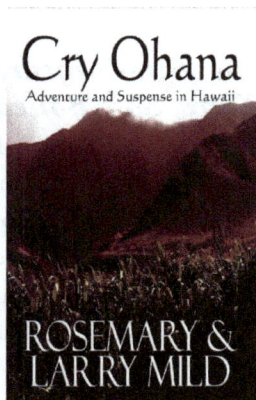

Honolulu Heat—Leilani and Alex Wong anguish over son Noah, an idealistic teenager who teeters on both sides of the law. He meets Nina Portfia, his dream girl, but they unwittingly share horrific secrets. Noah finds himself immersed in a bloody feud between a Chinatown protection racketeer and a crimeland don who, ironically, is Nina's father.

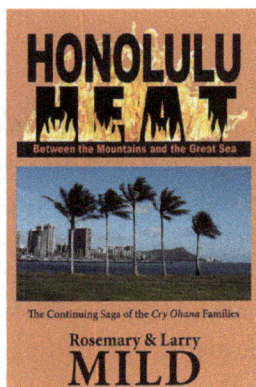

Available on Amazon.com and all e-readers.

Murder, Fantasy, and Weird Tales

—Delve into tales of the brave, the foolhardy, and the wicked on their journeys to the unknown in Hawai'i, Japan, Cambodia, Italy, and elsewhere. Art lovers, hit women, a vampire, a lively hologram, and others reveal their secret compulsions.

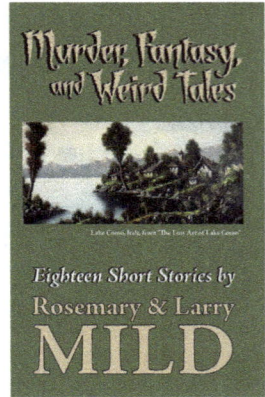

The Misadventures of Slim O. Wittz, Soft-Boiled Detective—"If

you're looking for a truly bumbling gumshoe, you want me, Slim. I'm frequently behind the eight ball and seldom paid. In eight complete mystery stories I always bump into criminals. And you're right: my case record is remarkably shaky."

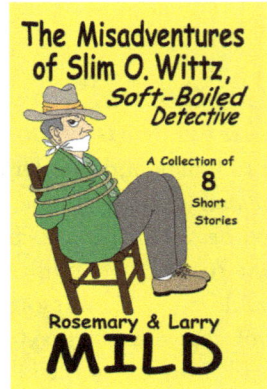

Copper and Goldie • 13 Tails of Adventure and Suspense in Hawaii

—Sam, a disabled cop, now a PI, and his canine sidekick, Goldie, ply the streets of Honolulu in a Checker Cab, looking for fares and solving all sorts of crimes they encounter. 13 exciting short story adventures.

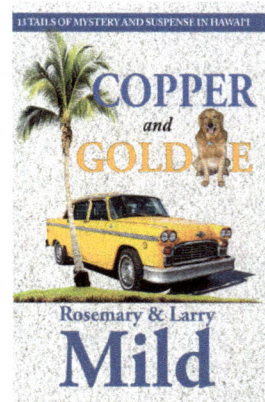

Available on Amazon.com and all e-readers.

Miriam's World—and Mine
—Miriam Luby Wolfe, a junior at Syracuse U., spent her fall semester in London exploring her talents: singing, dancing, acting, and writing. But she never made it home. A terrorist bomb destroyed her plane over Lockerbie, Scotland. Learn about Miriam, the Pan Am families, the bombers, and the political fallout.

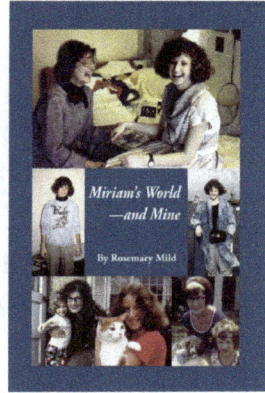

Love! Laugh! Panic! Life with My Mother—Don't we all have mixed emotions about our mothers? Rosemary Mild's mom was super-achieving, but tough to live with. Luby Pollack was a journalist, popular book author, and psychiatrist's wife. Always the heroine, and sometimes the villain, from the viewpoint of her loving but ornery daughter.

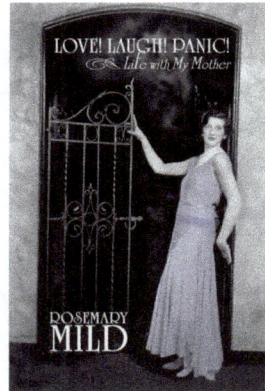

In My Next Life I'll Get It Right— is a collection of personal essays ranging from the hilarious to the serious—keen, sometimes wicked, observations on everyday life. And… wishful thinking mixed with tough reality, See how Rosemary views her two marriages, the good and the not so good. Join her as she takes on sailing, skating, Jazzercise, football, and more—and feel for a mother's heart-wrenching loss.

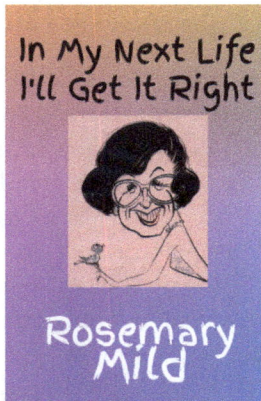

Available on Amazon.com and all e-readers.

Unto the Third Generation—Two young people, each unaware of the other, volunteer to become cryonauts—physically frozen in a life-suspension experiment. Leonard, a steel worker, and Francine, a waitress, postpone their destinies for untold generations. But their lives are in jeopardy —depending upon two world-shaking events.

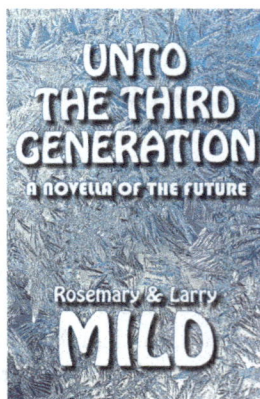

Charley and the Magic Jug and Other Short Stories—Climb the mountain to the secret cave with Charley. Watch three brothers face a sweet but certain death. Learn how a tiny pill can changes lives. Get away through time with thieves. See what the winds reveal in "Tsunami." Follow Casey as he chases the ladies in "On the Prowl." And witness so much more in a score of short stories

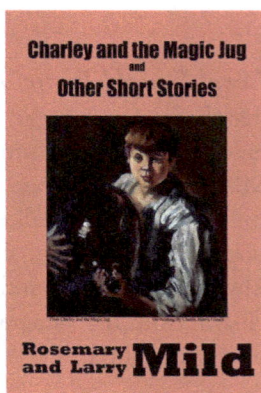

Also by Larry

No Place To Be But Here—It is not only Larry's own story, but that of his family. Join him as he tells how his two wives, three children, and five grandchildren have shaped his life as much as he has molded theirs. Tragedy is certainly no stranger as he deals with death, cancer, murder, and global terrorism, not only on the written page, but in his own life.

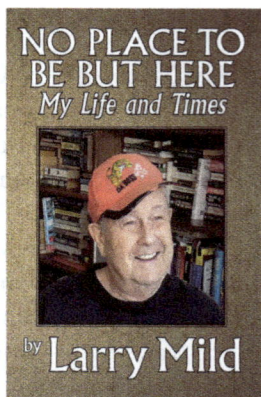

Available on Amazon.com and all e-readers.

www.ingramcontent.com/pod-product-compliance
Lightning Source LLC
Chambersburg PA
CBHW060317030426
42336CB00011B/1090